DEISM versus THEISM

2-7 in the Scientific Arena of the 20th Century

JULEON SCHINS

Deism Versus Theism
2-7 in the Scientific Arena
of the 20th Century

ISBN 978-1-64550-500-6 (Paperback)

CONTENTS

This book is part of a 2019 decalogue consisting of

- Sign of Times: Music Anthology and Lyric Analysis
- Hollywood Misogyny
- Beginners' Guide to the FED:
  Why it is Unique on our Planet
- The Kennedy Kurse: Four Obvious Konnektions
- Manichaeism and Satanic Child Abuse
- Progressive Intolerance: Last Stop Before Hitler
- Patriotic Ingenuousness
- Deism versus Theism:
  2-7 in the Scientific Arena of the 20th Century
- Feminine Feminist:
  A Missing Link Eluding Discovery
- The Snake: Three Millennia of Anti-Semitism

Dedicated to the Memory

of Austrian Dr. Kurt Gödel

THE Scientific Genius of the 20th century

INTRODUCTION
The Nine Big Bangs

Being a Theist myself, I prefer to have a Deist explain to the reader what deism is.[1]

"Deism is a philosophical belief that posits that God exists as an uncaused First Cause ultimately responsible for the creation of the universe, but does not interfere directly with the created world. Equivalently, deism can also be defined as the view which posits God's existence as the cause of all things, and admits its perfection (and usually the existence of natural law and Providence) but rejects divine revelation or

---

1   A selection of quotes from the Wikipedia page on Deism

direct intervention of God in the universe by miracles. It also rejects revelation as a source of religious knowledge and asserts that reason and observation of the natural world are sufficient to determine the existence of a single creator or absolute principle of the universe.

Deism is a theological theory concerning the relationship between a creator and the natural world. Deistic viewpoints emerged during the scientific revolution of 17th-century Europe and came to exert a powerful influence during the 18th-century Enlightenment. Deism stood between the narrow dogmatism of the period and skepticism. Though deists rejected atheism, they often were called "atheists" by more traditional theists. There were a number of different forms in the 17th and 18th centuries. In England, deists included a range of people from anti-Christian to non-Christian theists.

Deism gained prominence among intellectuals during the Age of Enlightenment, especially in Britain, France, Germany, and the United States. Typically, these had been raised as Christians and believed in one God, but they had become disenchanted with organized religion and orthodox teachings such as the Trinity, Biblical inerrancy, and the supernatural interpretation of events, such as miracles. Included in those influenced by its ideas were leaders of the American and French Revolutions. [...here follows a long complaint regarding theist attacks on deism....]

Enlightenment thinkers, under the influence of Newtonian science, tended to view the universe as a vast machine, created and set in motion by a creator being, that continues to operate according to natural law, without any divine intervention. This view naturally led to what was then usually called necessitarianism (the modern term is determinism): the view that everything in the universe —including human behavior— is completely causally determined by antecedent circumstances and natural law. (See, for example, L'Homme Machine by De La Mettrie.) As a consequence, debates about freedom versus necessity were a regular feature of Enlightenment religious and philosophical discussions.

Because of their high regard for natural law and for the idea of a universe without miracles, deists were especially susceptible to the temptations of determinism. Reflecting the intellectual climate of the time, there were differences among deists about freedom and determinism. Some, such as Anthony Collins, actually were determinists. Deists hold a variety of beliefs about the soul.

It is quite funny to read a Deist's complaints about Theism, as there does not exist a single Deist outside a traditionally Theist society. Requoting our Wiki-Deist: "Deism gained prominence among intellectuals during the Age of Enlightenment, especially in Britain, France, Germany, and the United States". No tiny spark here, Wiki-Deist? You mention four countries whose inhabitants have a millenarian history of Theism! So in what culture would Deism have made the least chance of propagation? In the Aztec possibly, or in the Assyrian? And if so, how does one explain that Deism *just happened to be born in a theist society?* Plain historical account and deism do not fit through the same door, apparently.

Isn't it a miracle that the bloodthirsty and Guillotine-driven French revolution, which ended in chaos, giving birth to dictator Mr. Napoléon from the anti-French Corsica, assumed as its emblem "liberté, égalité, fraternité"? Well, the miracle disappears upon translating "liberty, equality, and fraternity... for the new bourgeois class that takes over power from the old nobility and the Catholic Church". As I hope my dear Wiki-Deist knows, the terms "liberty, equality, and fraternity", *in their interwoven and universal[2] acceptance*, were first coined by a zeroth century semi-nomad called Mr. Jesus Nazarene, son of a Galilean carpenter. His viewpoint was —for some incomprehensible reason— firmly established inside the Roman Coliseum, by thousands of his followers. These had the choice between either abjuring their theist faith in the Nazarene being God Incarnate, or being fed to lions. During three centuries the Roman populace had a good laugh at watching Nazarene followers being torn to pieces, time and again. In spite of this granted treatment, an important minority of them neither hid, nor abjured. I am sorry to say so, but in Roman culture deism would not have lasted five minutes. And what brave people were the popularizers of the enlightened version of "liberté, égalité, fraternité"? Parasites like Voltaire, known for his vomiting "écrasez l'infâme!"[3]

So, my dear Deist, writer of the Wikipedia page, let me ask you: what was the reason that you did not manage to simply write that Deism had a strong anti-Theist

---

2 Very well-known are the Jewish restriction (only with respect to Jews) and the French revolutionary restriction (for all French except Catholics and Nobility).
3 French for "Pulverize the ignominious", obviously referring to the Catholic Church. Poor Voltaire was not able to force the word "Catholics" through his throat.

tendency from its very birth? This makes you a coward, in my perception. Let us not even talk about your specifying which specific theistic traits were not acceptable to Deists.

On the other hand, as far as I know, the Catholic Church never harmed a single Deist, and never issued a Muslim-like fatwa against deism. Individual Catholics may write what they wish: The Catholic Church takes responsibility only for her own writings. This is quite different in non-Christian cultures. As far as I know, there does not exist a single outspoken Deist in enlightened leftwing dictatorships (Hitler[4], Mussolini[5], Stalin, Mao,

---

4   Hitler was voted to power in what was called the "Nationalsozialistische Deutsche ArbeiterPartei", abbreviated NSDAP. Translated: the "German National-Socialistic Labor Party". The "z" in "Nazi" comes from the German "sozialistische", and obviously not from "National". Hitler's horror of Communists does not make him right–wing, given the world-wide socialist parties' feelings towards communism as mere competitors for votes. It makes him even less a fascist (a completely unknown phenomenon in 1940 Germany), but simply a socialist nut with too ambitious ideas: one of the increasingly many who come to power and turn into coward savages. Just have a look at Spanish national politics.

5   Mussolini was the true creator of fascism, and as history does not fail to show, Mussolini started out as a left-wing labor-party journalist, and never abjured of his left-wing roots. It is the enlightened left that indulged in massacring Jews, *not* the "traditional" right. Likewise, the German "traditional" Catholic south voted 100% against Hitler in 1933, and the "enlightened" north 100% in favor. Until voting was declared superfluous by decision of the German democracy, who preferred a tyranny over a democracy. Of course, with abundant help from Nazi terror. Why, then, was Pope XII

Pol-Pot, Ceaușescu, Win, Afewerki, and the still active Kim in North Korea).

Some thirteen centuries ago, Mr. Muhammad ibn Abdullāh from Mecca, a self-proclaimed prophet of god, allegedly visited many times by Archangel Gabriel, managed to bring a flourishing Arab society to a complete halt, blocking all intellectual growth, whether juridical, technical, social, medical, mathematical, or physical.

Result: Muslim society has been stalled from the 7th century until the 19th, when emigration began. Their only adaptation to the 21st century consists in the use of cars, TV's with parabolic antenna's pointing to Mecca, and mobile phones. Everywhere they go, the large majority keeps speaking their own language, because heathens' languages are filthy (by definition, as Gabriel spoke the language of the Quran). As they consider studying anything different from the Quran as a mere loss of time, they are able only to take on the humblest jobs, where they suffer unspeakable humiliations.

Only Muslim women living abroad seem to appreciate a few intellectual aspects from heathen-land. Some of them manage to make it to University, after which a life-

---

declared guilty after the second world war? These are higher EZ-like forces, which are not discussed in this book.

long familiar harassment begins, unless they decide to break with their family forever, and get involved with a heathen. The best-known champion of female rights in Muslim society is Ayaan Hirsi Ali.[6]

Muhammad ibn Abdullāh's legacy was a devastating decapitation: no more medical investigation (ended with Ibn al-Nafis, a 13th century Arab jurist-physician from Damascus, also known as ""the father of circulatory physiology"), no more philosophical investigation (ended with the 12th century Andalusian Ibn-Rushd, or Averroes), no more mathematical investigation (ended with Muhammad ibn Mūsā al-Khwārizmī, a 9th century Persian scholar, born in Khiva of the present-day Uzbekistan, who produced works in mathematics, astronomy, and geography under the patronage of Caliph Al-Ma'mun of

---

6   Ayaan Hirsi Ali is a Somali-born Dutch-American activist,
     feminist, author, scholar and former politician (until the
     Dutch left cowardly kicked her out for an alleged inaccuracy in
     her immigration papers). She received international attention
     as a critic of Islam and advocate for the rights and self-
     determination of Muslim women, actively opposing forced
     marriage, honor violence, child marriage and female genital
     mutilation. She has founded an organization for the defense of
     women's rights, the AHA Foundation. She is a Fellow with the
     Hoover Institution at Stanford University, a Fellow with the
     Future of Diplomacy Project at the Belfer Center for Science
     and International Affairs at The Harvard Kennedy School, a
     visiting scholar at the American Enterprise Institute in
     Washington, D.C., and a member of the Council on Foreign
     Relations. (from Wikipedia)

the Abbasid Caliphate) [7], and no more artistic innovation. Still today, only Muslims are capable of destroying age-old Buddha statues, or put a world-wide fatwa on Asia Bibi, without any significant protests from the Muslim society.

Even though the Islamic Sharia requires much less than the Christian Commandments,[8] cultures where deism was popular. Until the nineteenth century deism only flourished in (ex-)Christian societies. Its only reason of existence is criticizing selected Christian beliefs deism does not like, without adding anything positive in exchange — indeed, everything intellectual our Wiki-Deist claims (e.g., about natural law or philosophy), was common knowledge since the medieval Sorbonne professors Saint Albert the Great, and his disciple, Saint Thomas Aquinas. Instead of taking the pains of quoting the original Christian sources, our Wiki-Deist prefers to quote enlightened epigones who are mentally stuck in the French Monarchy of Mr. Capet, also known as King Louis XVI.

Whereas deism is both a philosophy and a theology (yes, you read me well, but I don't know better than

---

7   The terms algebra and algorithm, are both due to Mūsā al-
      Khwārizmī.
8   and the punishments are idiotic

keeping literally to the quote of our Wiki-Deist), theism is neither of them. It has nothing to do with philosophy, nor has it the least in common with theology. It is simply one of the infinitely many possible *interpretations of some very selected historical facts.*

This booklet contains nine chapters, which discuss as many basic discoveries of 20th century. The first eight chapters all study "Big Bangs", as they all refer to something totally new brought into existence. The cosmological Big Bang created the universe; the biological Big Bang the first self-replicating cell; the animal behavioral Big Bang animal behavior; the human behavioral Big Bang the human soul; the Danish Big Bang the left-wing interference with science; the quantum-mechanical Big Bang fundamental indeterminacy; the causal Big Bang necessary causality and human freedom; the number-theoretical Big Bang consistent incompleteness; and the shroud's Big Bang (treated in the Appendix) the proof of Christ's resurrection. The ninth chapter does not study a Big Bang, but a Big Crunch: that of the IPCC.

CHAPTER 1
Cosmology

The cosmological Big Bang was the work of many scientists, with an undoubtedly prime role for Georges Lemaître, and a second one for Albert Einstein. Some very clever deist physicists passed away, after having spent half their life to the "good cause". A magnificent example is Fred Hoyle, who on his death bed still swore on his "steady state" model of the universe. Meanwhile, all major experimental observations (most importantly, the so-called "3K-cosmic background radiation" observed by Penzias and Wilson in 1964, the distribution of young galaxies and quasars throughout the Universe in the 1980s, and the increasingly rapid expansion of our universe in the 2000's) proved him wrong, and Lemaître right. The latter was a poorly known Belgian physicist and Catholic priest, who first formulated the big bang solution to Einstein's general relativity equation.[9] The big bang was nothing but a possible solution of Einstein's equations, with a very peculiar initial condition: a singularity, marking the origin of time and space. His solution was not acceptable to the large majority of cosmologists, because the "initial singularity" reminded one immediately of the Catholic dogma of a divine act of creation "out of nothing". And modern science was no doubt on the verge of disclosing all crap issued by the Catholic Universal Councils, wasn't it?

The outspoken Deist, Einstein, abhorred the idea, too. In contrast to Hoyle, however, he was so wise to await some more experimental evidence. Moreover, he disliked Hoyle's steady state model even more than Lemaître's big bang. His many discussions with Lemaître finally convinced him to supporting the "big bang", although it

---

[9]   Lemaître's model was soon to be improved by the Odessa-born Atheist George Gamow. Gamow did this by assuming that the early universe was dominated by radiation rather than by matter. In 1953 he determined the density of the relict background radiation from which he predicted a thermal background radiation temperature of 7K (twice the presently known value). Both physicists are being struck out of history by the deist mafia.

broke his deist heart. The majority of cosmologists today still finds the "big bang" indigestible.

Some more words need be dedicated to Fred Hoyle. Most importantly, despite his stubbornness, or his abhorrence of theism, Fred Hoyle was not a quibbler as deist humanists, like philosophers or theologians. He was a genius who made impressive contributions to science. We review some of them in simple words; again, the basic ideas are taken from Wikipedia.

During the 1950's Hoyle worked for the British Admiralty on radar research. He managed to measure the altitude of nearby airplanes. He was also put in charge of countermeasures against the radar-guided torpedoes found on the German *Graf Spee*. His radar work allowed him to pay some scientific visits to the US and Canada, where he learned about supernovae and the nuclear physics of plutonium, both of which led to his original thoughts on "supernova nucleosynthesis". Supernova's are huge stars on the verge of exploding into radiation and cooler debris; and nucleosynthesis is a scientific term for the production of atomic nuclei from the fusion of helium atoms, the prime constituents of stellar matter.

The difference between an atom and an atomic nucleus is that the latter is neutral in charge, due to its surrounding electrons; or the other way round, an atomic nucleus is an atom stripped of all its electrons. Chemistry studies the behavior of outer electrons on otherwise neutral or slightly loaded molecules. Nuclear physics studies the behavior of neutrons and protons inside a nucleus. The smaller the sizes, the larger the energies involved. Nuclei are very compact in comparison with the diameters of electrons circling around them: for carbon, the atomic volume is about 10 to the power 22 times that of the nucleus.

Nuclei consist of protons and neutrons. These two have about the same mass, but protons have a positive charge, while neutrons are ... neutral, as their name betrays. Atoms are ordered according to their nuclear charge (also called "atomic number"), in so-called periodic tables. Figure 1.1 shows such a table, first devised by the Russian chemist Mendeleev.

In 1946 Hoyle showed that the cores of stars will evolve to temperatures of billions of degrees, much hotter than thought before. Under these conditions electrons are nothing but an inert soup with the only function of keeping the star electrically neutral. Hoyle showed that at such high temperatures iron nuclei can become much more abundant than even heavier nuclei owing to thermal equilibrium. This process explains the high natural abundance of iron with respect to all its neighbors at either side of magnitude. Obviously, Helium was and remains the most prominent nucleus in the universe.

©NCSSM 2002

Periodic Table of Elements
based on Mendeleev's Periodic Law

0	I / H 1.01	II	III	IV	V	VI	VII		VIII	
He 4.00	Li 6.94	Be 9.01	B 10.8	●C 12.0	N 14.0	O 16.0	F 19.0			
Ne 20.2	Na 23.0	Mg 24.3	Al 27.0	Si 28.1	P 31.0	●S 32.1	Cl 35.5			
Ar 40.0	K 39.1	Ca 40.1	Sc 45.0	Ti 47.9	V 50.9	Cr 52.0	Mn 54.9	●Fe 55.9	Co 58.9	Ni 58.7
	●Cu 63.5	Zn 65.4	Ga 69.7	Ge 72.6	As 74.9	Se 79.0	Br 79.9			
Kr 83.8	Rb 85.5	Sr 87.6	Y 88.9	Zr 91.2	Nb 92.9	Mo 95.9	Tc (99)	Ru 101	Rh 103	Pd 106
	●Ag 108	Cd 112	In 115	●Sn 119	Sb 122	Te 128	I 127			
Xe 131	Ce 133	Ba 137	●La 139	Hf 179	Ta 181	W 184	Re 180	Os 194	Ir 192	Pt 195
	●Au 197	●Hg 201	Ti 204	●Pb 207	Bi 209	Po (210)	At (210)			
Rn (222)	Fr (223)	Ra (226)	●Ac (227)	●Th 232	●Pa (231)	●U 238				

Lanthanide series
● Actinide series

▨ Dobereiner's triads ▢ Known to Mendeleev ● Known to Ancients

Figure 1.1: Mendeleev's Periodic Table of Elements. The essence of the Table is its threefold organization: the atomic number, the row, and the column.[10]

Hoyle's second foundational nucleosynthesis publication showed that the elements between carbon and iron (see Fig. 1: N, O, F, Ne, Na, Mg, Al, Si, P, S, Cl, Ar, K, Ca, Sc, Ti, V, Cr, and Mn) cannot be synthesized equilibrium fusion

---

10 The atomic number is the order of appearance, and identical to the number of protons in the nucleus; the column counts the number of outer shell electrons; and the row indicates the number of completely filled electron shells. For example, the first element, hydrogen (H), consists of a single proton and no neutron (ergo, mass=1). The second element, helium (He), consists of 2 protons and 2 neutrons (ergo, mass=4).

processes in hot helium: since iron is the most stable
nucleus, spontaneous fusion (with emission of heat) only
works from lighter to heavier elements (with respect to
iron), and likewise, spontaneous fission[11] only works from
heavier to lighter elements. He attributed those elements
to specific nuclear fusion reactions between abundant
constituents in concentric shells of evolved massive, pre-
supernova stars.

Moreover, Hoyle proposed an explanation for the
abundance of carbon in solar systems. Life on earth is
carbon-based, as one may deduce from the overall diet-
word "hydro-carbon": the fundamental ingredient of
bread and sugar. Without a proper explanation of the
origin of carbon, it is simply impossible to give reason of
biology as we know it. Hoyle calculated a specific "nuclear
path" that fuses three helium nuclei into a single carbon
nucleus at sufficiently high rates. His calculations had
quite restricting consequences for the physical properties
of the produced carbon nucleus.[12] Experiments later
confirmed Hoyle's predictions to the last tiny detail.

---

11   Nuclear fusion is the process in which two separate nuclei
      melt into a single nucleus; nuclear fission is the opposite
      process, in which a single nucleus breaks up into two lighter
      nuclei. The best-known fission elements are uranium and
      plutonium.
12   To wit: the nuclear ground state energy of carbon, its nuclear
      spin and nuclear parity

Hoyle may have been a stubborn self-proclaimed atheist, but he was not sectarian. About not-god he wrote:

> Would you not say to yourself, "Some super-calculating intellect must have designed the properties of the carbon atom, otherwise the chance of my finding such an atom through the blind forces of nature would be utterly minuscule. A common sense interpretation of the facts suggests that a super-intellect has monkeyed with physics, as well as with chemistry and biology, and that there are no blind forces worth speaking about in nature. The numbers one calculates from the facts seem to me so overwhelming as to put this conclusion almost beyond question."[13]

This statement allows for a simpler paraphrase: God exists, He made both natural law, and the matter that obeys this natural law.

Else, what could be his "super-intellect"? Did it only monkey with mathematics? That might explain why all matter behaves conform to mathematical laws, but it does

---

[13]   Fred Hoyle, "The Universe: Past and Present Reflections." Engineering and Science, November, 1981.

not explain the origin of matter itself. You can hardly expect it to issue from a math-monkeying super-intellect. Clearly, Hoyle mistook "being an atheist" for "being a scientist who considers science an autonomous discipline". His language and statements are 100% deist. What seems a deist because it talks like one and thinks like one, most probably... *is* one.[14]

From the above statement one can deduce directly that it was not God's *creating our universe* that bothered him so much in Lemaître's big bang, but God's *creating it with boundary conditions far beyond human comprehension.*

Another famous statement of Fred Hoyle shows his scientific integrity: [15]

If one proceeds directly and straightforwardly in this matter, without being deflected by a fear of incurring the wrath of scientific opinion, one arrives at the conclusion that biomaterials with their amazing measure of order must be the

---

14   One might ask: what motivated Hoyle's atheist self-
      proclamation? I guess it is plain shame, not to be taken
      seriously by his equally ashamed colleagues
15   Fred Hoyle, "Evolution from Space", Omni Lecture, Royal
      Institution, London, 12 January 1982

outcome of intelligent design. No other possibility
I have been able to think of...

In close cooperation with Chandra Wickramasinghe,[16]
Hoyle calculated that the chance of obtaining the required
set of enzymes for even the simplest living cell without
panspermia[17] was one in 10 to the power 40,000. Since
the number of atoms in the known universe is totally
negligible (10 to the power 80), he argued that Earth as
life's place of origin could be ruled out. Remember, these
powers can be confusing. Upon multiplying the number
of atoms in our universe by 10, the result is 10 to the
power 81, which is just as negligible. One needs not the
actual number of atoms multiplied *once* by 10, nor *twice*,
nor *thrice*, but *39,920 times* by 10.

---

16   Chandra Wickramasinghe was a Sri Lankan-born British
      mathematician, astronomer and astrobiologist of Sinhalese
      ethnicity
17   Panspermia is the process in which biological life starts in the
      universe (outside our planet) and spreads through the
      universe. Probability arguments convinced Hoyle to reject
      "abiogenesis", the supposition that planet earth is the only
      origin of biological life. With Wickramasinghe, Hoyle
      promoted the idea that evolution on Earth is influenced by a
      steady influx of viruses arriving via comets. His belief that
      comets had a significant percentage of organic compounds
      was well ahead of his time, as the dominant views in the 1970s
      and 1980s were that comets largely consisted of water-ice, and
      the presence of organic compounds was then highly
      controversial.

The notion that not only the biopolymer but the operating program of a living cell could be arrived at by chance in a primordial organic soup here on the Earth is evidently nonsense of a high order.[18]

His is also the well-known comparison that the random emergence of even the simplest cell on earth to the likelihood that "a tornado sweeping through a junkyard might assemble a Boeing 747 from the materials therein" and to compare the chance of obtaining even a single functioning protein by chance combination of amino acids to "a solar system full of blind men solving Rubik's Cubes simultaneously".

A clear 0-1 for deism versus theism, methinks, due to a shot on own goal by deism. There was not the least reason for deism to embrace steady states just because deism wants its god distant and unknowable. Well, distant He is, as the universe started 13.8 billion years ago, our solar system 4.5 billion years ago, and carbon-based mono-cellular life 4 billion years ago.

But unknowable...

---

18   That is, of the order 40.000. For all details, see
      https://en.wikipedia.org/wiki/Fred_Hoyle

Chapter 2

Biology
Origin of the first self-replicating cell

2.1 Hoyle's Second Big Bang

As you might well know, Fred Hoyle made a name in astronomy by coining the term "Big Bang" in order to ridicule Lemaître's theory on the beginning of the universe,.[19] Today it is firmly established that Lemaître was right. Nonetheless, Hoyle remains a scientist with an outstanding record on many different scientific fields. In one of those fields, the origin of life,[20] he speculated on a

---

19   This term was no doubt meant disparagingly. Today, however, it has turned into the slogan of the prior underdog.
20   He did throw himself onto the most difficult questions: the origin of different physical processes. That makes him a very courageous, though somewhat stubborn and haughty scientist.

theory called "panspermia". While his first posture was taken on mere ideological grounds (he did not like the direct reference to a Creator God), his posture on the origin of life was based on probability calculations.

His statements about the first cell are no exaggerations. Actually, the creation of biological life on earth (the first cell) is no less a divine miracle than that of the universe. Without knowing that himself, Hoyle identified the second big bang, that of the origin of biological life!

2.2 An Extremely Short Introduction into Molecular Biology

In order to get an ever so slight feeling about this second big bang, let us just look at how atoms are ordered in biological life. Proteins are very specific series of amino-acids. Biologic life heavily depends on the 21 amino-acids, as they are the building elements of every functioning protein. A protein does in a cell what a robot does in an automatized factory: the essential and heavy work. They are carbon-based chains themselves, as is obvious from Fig. 2.1.[21] Likewise, DNA (across all animals, humans

---

21   https://en.wikipedia.org/wiki/Amino_acid

included) is a double chain of "nuclear acids"[22] of which there are only four kinds (see Fig. 2.2):[23] Adenine, Cytosine, Guanine, and Thymine, made up of carbon, nitrogen, oxygen, and hydrogen. The structure of the corresponding molecules is shown around their initials (A, C, G, T). The backbone has three functions: to keep the nuclear acids ordered, to configure a mirroring half strain to produce exclusively AC or GT bonds, thus forming the well-known double-helix DNA molecule.

Every unnamed site represents a carbon atom with as many hydrogen atoms as to achieve four electronic bonds. In every amino-acid one can identify a "carbon-only" backbone. The Wiki-author of this figure even took the pains to illustrate which bonds are "out-of-plane" (triangle) and which are "in-plane" (strict lines). The lines inside a hexagon or pentagon indicate what chemists call "resonances". They are meant to comply with the four-electron "coordination" rule, which allows the reader to easily deduce the number of hydrogen atoms involved.

---

22   The word "nuclear" in cosmology and high-energy physics has nothing whatsoever in common with the word "nuclear" in biology.
23   https://en.wikipedia.org/wiki/Nuclear_acid

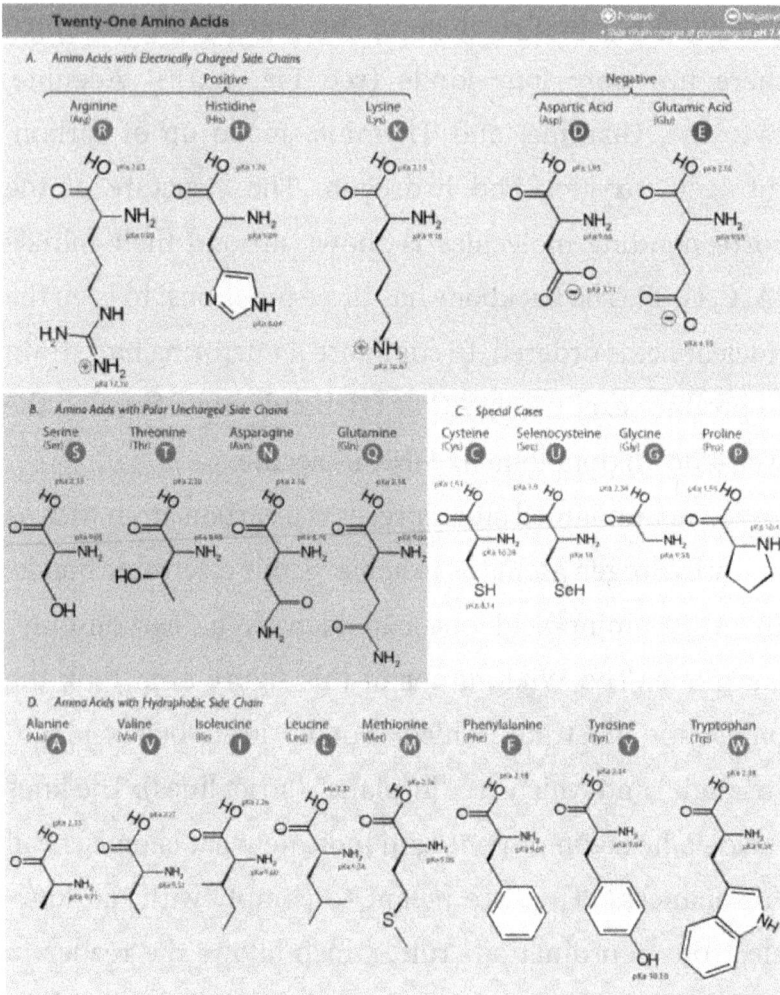

Figure 2.1: The 21 amino-acids
common to all living beings.

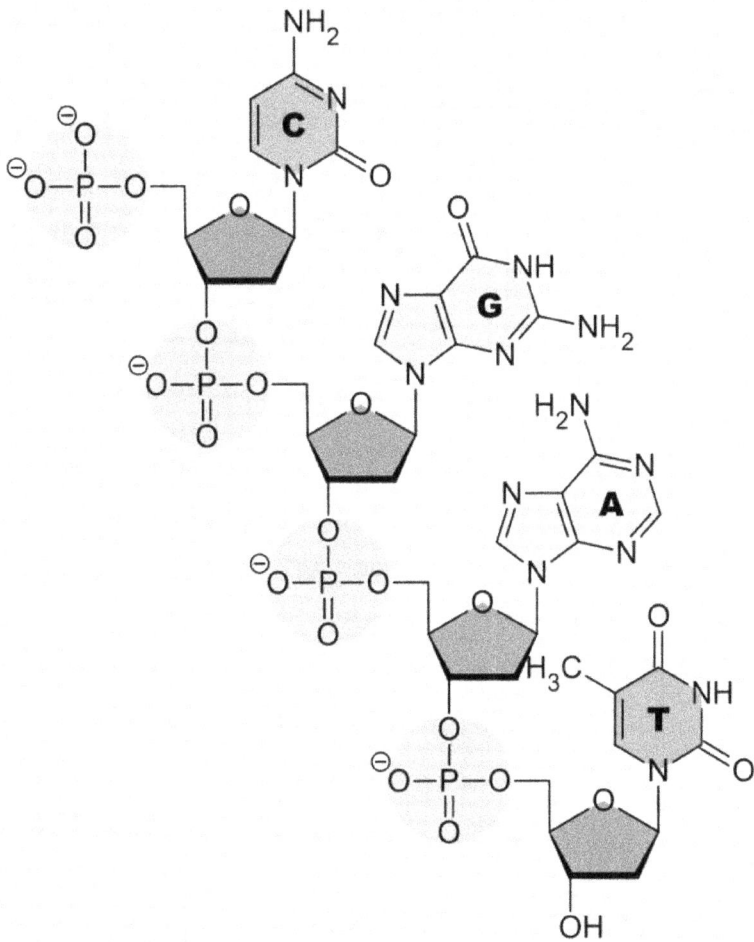

Figure 2.2: Nucleic Acids. The four only nucleic acids in biological DNA are A, C, G, T. The helix backbone consists of a chain of alternating phosphate groups and sugars. The phosphate group consists of a central phosphor atom surrounded by four oxygen atoms. The sugar molecule is "deoxyribose": A C_4O pentagon with an OH branch.

2.3 Descartes, Mendel and Darwin

Finally, deism had something in hand which held the promise of a strong determinist card! The first modern scientist who suspected that life was nothing but the property of an ingeniously built device was René Descartes [Méditations VI]:

"And as a clock composed of wheels and weights observes not less exactly all the laws of nature when it is ill-made and does not tell the hours as well as when it is entirely to the wish of the workman, so in like manner I regard the human body as a machine so built and put together of bone, nerve, muscle, vein, blood and skin, that still, although it had no mind, it would not fail to move in all the same ways as at present, since it does not move by the direction of its will, nor consequently by means of the mind, but only by the arrangement of its organs."

Descartes compared the intricate processes undergirding life with the complex machinery needed to keep a clock's minute hand moving around steadily. De La Mettrie, the French writer of "The machine-man", made the scientific arrogance-slash-ignorance of his time a laughing stock.

Yet Descartes' original idea contained a lot of truth. It took more than three centuries before Descartes' intuition received any significant scientific underpinning.

Celebrities like Gregor Mendel and Charles Darwin did the early pioneering work. In 1944 it was shown that the transfer of chromosomes (DNA in its closely packaged form) between different strains of bacteria also transferred heritable properties.[24] However, not all scientists accepted this experimental result, because they did not know of any kind of molecule —apart from proteins— complex enough to carry significant amounts of information. A very reasonable appreciation, in that time. But, the earthquake did not fail to come: The Franklin-Watson-Crick double helix shown in Fig. 2.3.

The perspectives on the left hand side are obtained by turning those on the right hand side by 90°, clockwise around the G-to-C axis. The dots connecting purines and pyrimidines at three (for CG) respectively two (for AT) sites are the "hydrogen bridges" mentioned in the text.

Further research definitively confirmed the supposition that DNA molecules carry hereditary

---

24   B. Alberts, D. Bray, J. Lewis, M. Raff, K. Roberts, and J.D.
      Watson, *Molecular biology of the cell*, Garland Publishing,
      New York NY 1995

information *throughout earthly life, not only among*
humans.

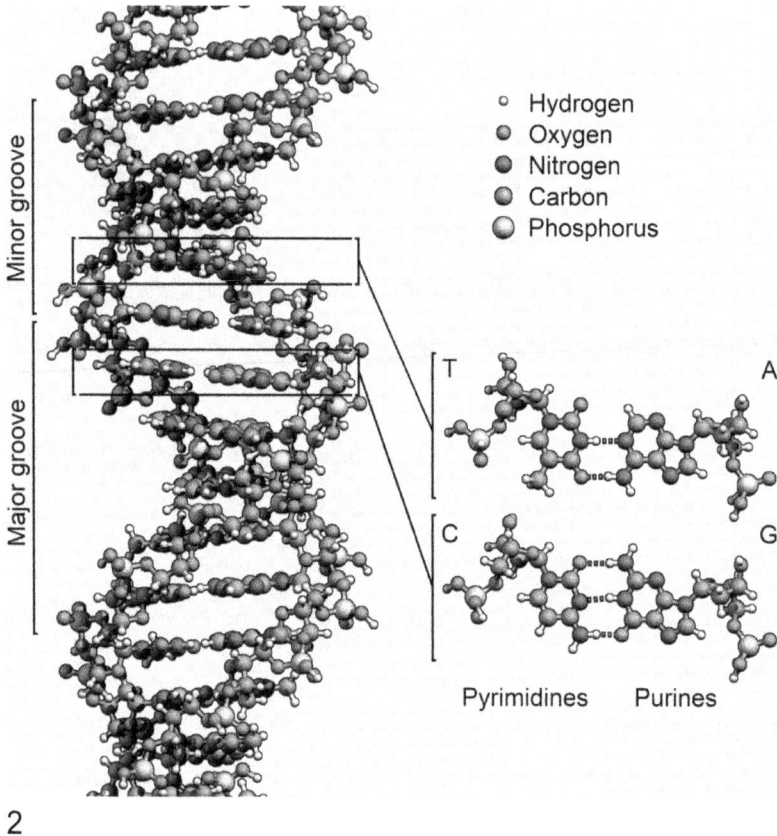

Fig. 2.3: The Double-Helix Structure of DNA.

This was definitive proof for Darwin's evolution theory.
Remember Fred Hoyle? However, that first self-
multiplying cell appeared on earth about four billion years
ago, Hoyle's 1 in 10 to the power 40.000 estimation totally

prohibited a second appearance elsewhere. Hoyle would consider just one living cell an anti-scientific miracle. He was right. There is no other scientific way to explain that all presently known life on earth is carbon-based, amino-based, and nucleic-acid-based. If a cow's life was silicon-based, how could humans ever profit from drinking her milk or eating her cheese?

The only way to appreciate the enormous organized complexity to build several species from a single cell, is to read a cellular biology text-book. I will do my best to offer the reader a glimpse into that scientific discipline.

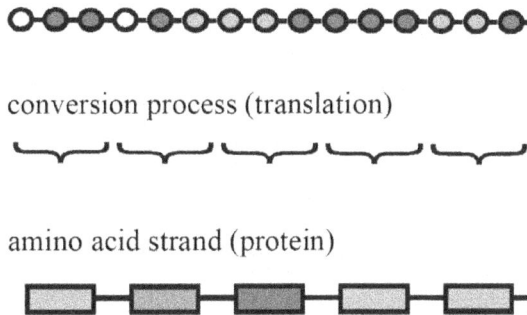

conversion process (translation)

amino acid strand (protein)

Figure 2.4: Translation of DNA triplets into amino acids in a complex process called "translation".

In reality, a double-helix DNA strand is first replicated into an "mRNA" single strand, which is then consumed on constructing the protein (a single, non-helix chain of amino acids, which take their natural form upon folding).

Three adjacent DNA nucleic acids form a 'codon', which cellular machinery (whose structure is encoded in DNA strings, like everything else in a biological cell) associates with an amino acid. The work of this machinery is called "translation" in biology. The machine is called *ribosome*, and is shown schematically in Fig. 2.5.[25] Its bottom part (small subunit) is mostly RNA-assembled, while the upper part (large subunit) mainly consists of proteins.

2.4 What came first: RNA or proteins?

The first big question for biologists is to unravel what came first: RNA or proteins. The problem is that with RNA alone one has a huge room of memory tapes, but no computer to read the information and process it. On the other hand, with proteins alone one has all computers in perfect shape, though without a code to execute. In both cases there is no output at all. Let alone, a replica of a protein. Messenger RNA (mRNA) is a single helix like that shown in Fig. 2.2, though with the nucleic acid Thymine replaced by Uracyl. It carries the same information as the

---

25   Both Tables 2.5 and 2.6 are taken from Wikipedia.

DNA string. It enters ribosome just in between the small (dark green, below) and the large (light green, above) subunits. A loaded transfer RNA molecule (tRNA) enters the large ribosome subunit from above. If its bottom part binds to the next mRNA triplet, it is promoted to the A-site, which is close to the end of the newly born protein.

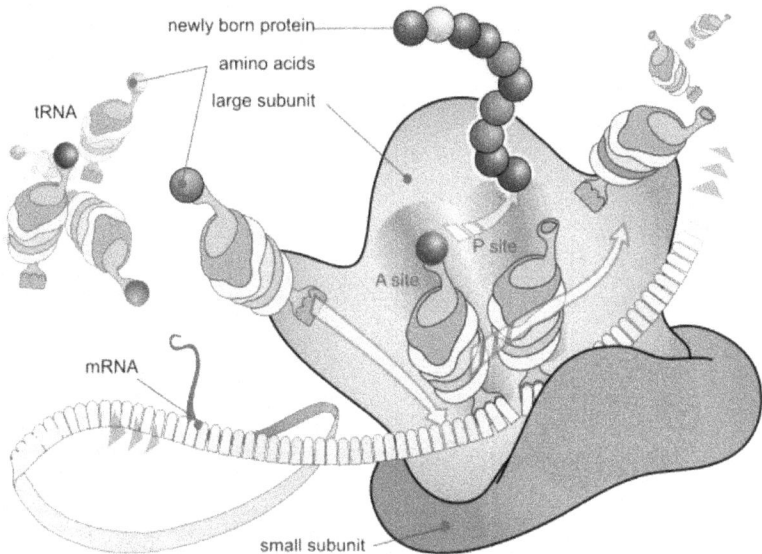

Figure 2.5: The Ribosome

The close proximity of the two amino acids, in combination with the ribosomal structure, pulls the tRNA molecule into the B-site, where the tRNA is loosed from its amino acid, and the bond between bottom tRNA and the mRNA triplet is broken.

Amino acids biochemical properties: nonpolar | polar | basic | acidic   Termination: stop codon

Standard genetic code

1st base	2nd base T	2nd base C	2nd base A	2nd base G	3rd base
T	TTT (Phe/F) Phenylalanine	TCT (Ser/S) Serine	TAT (Tyr/Y) Tyrosine	TGT (Cys/C) Cysteine	T
	TTC (Phe/F) Phenylalanine	TCC (Ser/S) Serine	TAC (Tyr/Y) Tyrosine	TGC (Cys/C) Cysteine	C
	TTA (Leu/L) Leucine	TCA (Ser/S) Serine	TAA Stop (Ochre) [B]	TGA Stop (Opal) [B]	A
	TTG (Leu/L) Leucine	TCG (Ser/S) Serine	TAG Stop (Amber) [B]	TGG (Trp/W) Tryptophan	G
C	CTT (Leu/L) Leucine	CCT (Pro/P) Proline	CAT (His/H) Histidine	CGT (Arg/R) Arginine	T
	CTC (Leu/L) Leucine	CCC (Pro/P) Proline	CAC (His/H) Histidine	CGC (Arg/R) Arginine	C
	CTA (Leu/L) Leucine	CCA (Pro/P) Proline	CAA (Gln/Q) Glutamine	CGA (Arg/R) Arginine	A
	CTG (Leu/L) Leucine	CCG (Pro/P) Proline	CAG (Gln/Q) Glutamine	CGG (Arg/R) Arginine	G
A	ATT (Ile/I) Isoleucine	ACT (Thr/T) Threonine	AAT (Asn/N) Asparagine	AGT (Ser/S) Serine	T
	ATC (Ile/I) Isoleucine	ACC (Thr/T) Threonine	AAC (Asn/N) Asparagine	AGC (Ser/S) Serine	C
	ATA (Ile/I) Isoleucine	ACA (Thr/T) Threonine	AAA (Lys/K) Lysine	AGA (Arg/R) Arginine	A
	ATG[A] (Met/M) Methionine	ACG (Thr/T) Threonine	AAG (Lys/K) Lysine	AGG (Arg/R) Arginine	G
G	GTT (Val/V) Valine	GCT (Ala/A) Alanine	GAT (Asp/D) Aspartic acid	GGT (Gly/G) Glycine	T
	GTC (Val/V) Valine	GCC (Ala/A) Alanine	GAC (Asp/D) Aspartic acid	GGC (Gly/G) Glycine	C
	GTA (Val/V) Valine	GCA (Ala/A) Alanine	GAA (Glu/E) Glutamic acid	GGA (Gly/G) Glycine	A
	GTG (Val/V) Valine	GCG (Ala/A) Alanine	GAG (Glu/E) Glutamic acid	GGG (Gly/G) Glycine	G

Table 2.6: Conversion Table from Ordered Triplet (DNA Codon) to Amino-Acid

The unloaded tRNA swims back to its loading station, another ribosome-like molecule, that manages to bind it to the specific amino acid (the loading process).

The superscript [A] at ATG means that the mRNA's AUG also codes for conversion initiation. It does not stop to startle: all amino-acids but Tryptophan and Methionine have more than two codons, and on the other hand, the codon ATG codes for two different operations. Change a single letter in this table, and life is not possible as we know it.

Triplets of four nucleic acids give rise to $4^3 = 64$ different directed triplets or "codons". Since nature uses only 20 different amino acids, there is an obvious redundancy in the coding, as can be appreciated from Table 2.6.

Of course, René Descartes had no inkling of the informational aspects of life, but after all this time it turns out that even the tiniest details of biological life reduce to complex machinery. Hence, in this respect he was a true prophet (in many others he was not, specifically regarding his philosophical writings, which go unnoticed among the average deistic nonsense).

The shape of protein assemblies is often hardly distinguishable from engineers' constructs. It makes one wonder whether blind selection is sufficient to account for their origin. As long as humankind does not witness heavy storms producing effective machinery from a junk yard, they will not witness the birth of a new cell from a primordial soup stricken by lightning, either. No doubt the best choice is to accept "variation and selection" as a biological misnomer for statistical physics, as proposed by Michael Behe.[26] He suggests that only intelligent programming, not blind selection, can produce something functional in biology. The sour truth is that "selection" of the pioneering biologists had already been studied for a century in physics, though on a scientific level. The biological term "selection" is a mere tautology. Change the environment, and the strong species will exchange roles with the weak one. The same occurs with "variation". In the mouth of a biologist like Dawkins,[27] selection is never blind, else the probabilities explode to Hoyle levels.

---

26   M. Behe, 1996, *Darwin's Black Box.*
27   R. Dawkins, *The Selfish Gene*, Oxford University Press, Oxford UK, 1976. Richard Dawkins says it very frankly in an interview in Japan: "The idea of *The Selfish Gene* is not mine, but I've done the most to sell it, and I've developed the rhetoric of it. The notion is implicit in the approach of the turn-of-the-century biologist August Weismann and in the neo-Darwinian synthesis of the 1930s. The idea was carried forward in the 1960s by W.D. Hamilton (then in London, now my colleague at Oxford) and by George C. Williams, at Stony Brook. My contribution to the idea of the selfish gene was to put rhetoric into it and spell out its implications."

2.5 Dawkins' Ridiculous Proposal

What Dawkins did discover himself, the so-called fruit-machine *simile* of evolution, represents a fruit-machine "DNA string" that at every run varies *only the "bad" nucleic acids,* that is to say, those parts which differ from the ideal DNA string. First: who or what knows how that ideal string should look like, the dinosaur itself possibly? Second, if the dinosaur did know, how would he do the job, in such a way, that the genetic changes are taken over by the next generation? I guess no serious deist biologist was ever so ashamed of a colleague's proposal!

Moreover, one cannot possibly deny that an enormous part of the cell's machinery is dedicated to correcting translation errors. Deism has not yet come up with a single example where variation without intelligent, continuous correction gave rise to something functional and new: In Dawkins' model all biological life would immediately degrade to cancer. No matter how complex biological information might be, it does not invalidate Descartes' fundamental intuition: a biological organism is nothing but a self-cloning factory. Both need a master plan steering the internal processes, both need complex machinery to perform highly specialized tasks.

unicellular organism	self-cloning factory
Chromosomes	Software
proteins	assembly robots
food	raw material
Excrements	waste
offspring	produced clones
Environment	program input
behaviour	program output
behavioural richness	problem-solving capacity

Table 2.7: Basic analogy between a unicellular organism and a self-cloning factory. The last three analogies are explained in Chapter 3.

Deism again lost a scientific earthquake (of explaining the appearance of the first cell and, possibly of novel species, too) to theism, thereby leaving the score on 0-2.

CHAPTER 3

Animal Behavior

3.1 Insect Behavior

The idea that physical laws, together with variation and selection (already accounted for in those laws, of course) dictate the evolution of behavior, including those strongly anthropomorphic aspects like altruism, care, intimacy, and the like, is generally regarded as a major achievement of Neo-Darwinism. The road was prepared by Fisher's "Genetic Theory of Natural Selection" written in 1930 and by Haldane's theory of population genetics dating of 1955. The definitive proof that a wide spectrum of anthropomorphic behavior is reducible to natural laws was provided in Hamilton's "Genetic Evolution of Social Behavior" in 1964. Hamilton explained altruism among insects like Hymenoptera on purely genetic grounds. It is worthwhile to take a close look at Hamilton's argument, as popularized by Richard Dawkins:[28]

"Insects of the group known as the Hymenoptera, including ants, bees, and wasps, have a very odd system of sex determination. Termites do not belong to this group and they do not share the same peculiarity. A hymenopteran nest typically has only one mature queen. She made one mating flight when young and stored up the sperms for the rest of her long life — ten years or even longer. She rations the sperms out to her eggs over the years, allowing the eggs to be fertilized as they pass out through her tubes. But not all the eggs are fertilized. The unfertilized ones develop into males. A male therefore has no father, and all the cells of his body contain just a single set of chromosomes (all obtained from his mother) instead of a double set (one from the father and one from the mother) as in ourselves. (...)

A female hymenopteran, on the other hand, is normal in that she does have a father, and she has the usual double set of chromosomes in each of

28 R. Dawkins, *The Selfish Gene*, Oxford University Press, Oxford UK, 1976

her body cells. Whether a female develops into a worker or a queen depends not on her genes but on how she is brought up. That is to say, each female has a complete set of queen-making genes, and a complete set of worker-making genes (or, rather, sets of genes for making each specialized caste of worker, soldier, etc.). Which set of genes is 'turned on' depends on how the female is reared, in particular on the food she receives. (...) Let us now try to calculate the relatedness between a mother and a son. If a male is known to possess a gene A, what are the chances that his mother shares it? The answer must be 100 per cent, since the male had no father and obtained all his genes from his mother. But now suppose a queen is known to have the gene B. The chance that her son shares the gene is only 50 per cent, since he contains only half her genes. (...) From a queen's point of view therefore, her offspring, of either sex, are as closely related to her as human children are to their mother. Things start to get intriguing when we come to sisters. Full sisters not only share the same father: the two sperms that conceived them were identical in every gene. The sisters are therefore equivalent to identical twins as far as their parental genes are concerned. If one female has gene A, she must have got it from either her father or her mother.

If she got it from her mother, then there is a 50 per cent chance that her sister shares it. But if she got it from her father, the chances are 100 per cent that her sister shares it. Therefore, the relatedness between hymenopteran full sisters is not $\frac{1}{2}$ as it would be for normal sexual animals, but $\frac{3}{4}$. It follows that a hymenopteran female is more closely related to her full sister than she is to her offspring of either sex. As Hamilton realized (though he did not put it in quite the same way) this might well predispose a female to farm her own mother as an efficient sister-making machine. A gene for vicariously making sisters replicates itself more rapidly than a gene for making offspring directly. Hence worker sterility evolved. It is presumably no accident that true sociality, with worker sterility, seems to have evolved no fewer than eleven times independently in the Hymenoptera and only once in the whole of the rest of the animal kingdom, namely in the termites."

Hamilton was the first to understand that complex social behavior, like the origin of worker sterility among hymenoptera, follows directly from the genes. Genes are nothing but self-cloning machines, and those genes survive that give rise to the highest replication efficiency.

This struggle for self-propagation is highly complex because a single gene depends on many others for its propagation. Hamilton was the first to understand that genes are the primary subjects of evolutionary selection, while organisms only act as their vehicles.

In 1976 Trivers and Hare argued that, based on Fisher's and Hamilton's theories, the genes of the queen strive for a sex ratio in her offspring of 1:1 while the genes of the female, sterile workers strive for a sex ratio in the queen's offspring of 3:1. These ratios are determined simply by the queen's chances of propagating a given gene to son or daughter (50%:50%=1:1), and by the gene overlap probability between a sterile worker and her sister or brother (75%:25%=3:1). Queen and workers are continually taking measures and counter-measures in order to influence the offspring ratio. Actually, this is an anthropomorphism: neither queen nor workers do anything, but their genes, subject to natural law.

Having studied twenty species of ants, Trivers and Hare found a close fit to the 3:1 female to male ratio, predicted when the workers win the sex-ratio battle with the queen.[29] Looking at two more ant species, of the slave-making kind, they found a sex ratio of 1:1, in agreement

---

29   R.L. Trivers and H. Hare, Haplodiploidy and the evolution of the social insects, Science **191**, 1976

with the queen's endeavor, because slaves do not 'know' the ins and outs of the slave-making brood. The successful description of altruism and sex ratios in Hymenoptera represents one of the most spectacular triumphs of what Dawkins later popularized as the 'selfish gene' theory. This theory is extremely sober and elegant, in that it completely dispenses with conscious intentionality.

3.2 Game Theory

Another field of research stressing the machine-like origin of altruistic behavior is game theory. In 1981 Robert Axelrod applied the fundamental principles of game theory to the evolution of co-operation, *also in situations where kinship does not play a role*.[30] In an important paper Axelrod and Hamilton give many examples of how a few elementary rules can give rise to complex strategies.[31] The rules are inspired by the 'prisoner's dilemma': if the prisoner co-operates with the plans of his buddy, two things can happen: both might escape from prison, or his buddy might betray him to the guards, in

---

30   R. Axelrod, *Effective choice in the prisoner's dilemma*, Journal of Conflict Resolution **24,** 1980
31   R. Axelrod and W.D. Hamilton, *The evolution of cooperation*, Science **211,** 1981

the hope of remission for good conduct. On the other hand, if the prisoner simulates co-operation, but betrays his buddy, the options are the following: either he obtains remission for good conduct, or, if his buddy betrays him too, both get punished. Such a situation can be summed up using only four numbers: the reward for mutual co-operation (both leave the prison), the reward for defection when buddy co-operates (remission for good conduct), the punishment for trying to escape when buddy betrays (sucker's payoff), and the punishment for mutual defection.

| | Player B | |
	Cooperates	Defects
Cooperates	mutual cooperation	sucker's pay-off
Defects	deception	mutual defection

Player A

Table 3.1: The Prisoner's Dilemma game from the point of view of Player A

The numerical values, chosen for the four parameters in a realistic simulation, satisfy the rule deception>mutual cooperation>0>mutual defection>sucker's pay-off, for player A. Therefore, in the simplest model, both players would obviously defect by principle. However, the introduction of memory and social interaction changes such choice quite a bit. The reader should be warned that these models depend on only six parameters, which are nothing but fit parameters, as nobody knows how to calculate theses parameters from genetic information.

Depending on the fit parameters, prisoners will adopt different strategies. These strategies have different degrees of stability against mutants. Mutants are organisms with slightly different behavior (fit parameters). When a stable pattern of behavior changes due to the introduction of a small number of mutants into the society, the strategy is unstable. If the pattern of behavior persists, then the prevailing strategy is stable.

Using Table 3.1, computers can be of help for mimicking strategies. The game level in nature obviously depends on the behavioral richness of the species involved. Fig trees cannot possibly tell one wasp from another; hence, their retaliation must necessarily be collective. On the other hand, bats are able to tell one individual from another,[32] giving rise to co-operative behavior.

---

32   E.A. Fisher, The relationship between mating system and
      simultaneous hermaphroditism in the coral reef fish

Behavioral richness of genomes is paralleled by the problem-solving capacity of software programs, just as the behavior of an individual in given circumstances is paralleled by the output of a program for a given input. Without knowing the details of a given program, it is certainly not possible to predict how changes in the source are going to influence the output of the program. Small changes in the software may entail huge changes in the output, and vice versa. Yet it is possible to formulate general rules when we consider only commercial programs, that is, programs that have survived the 'struggle for life' on a healthy, free market. Three hand-waving software rules for commercial programs are:

- programs differing little in code differ little in problem-solving capacity;
- programs differing much in problem-solving capacity differ much in code;
- programs with equal problem-solving capacity may differ much in code.

These rules reflect the following three hand-waving rules of behavioral richness:

Hypoplectrus nigricans Serranidae, Animal Behavior **28**, 1980, p. 620-633

- genetically similar organisms differ little in behavioral richness;
- organisms differing much in behavioral richness differ much genetically;
- organisms with equal behavioral richness may differ much genetically.

The data furnished in the Table 3.2 confirm the similarity. The table indicates on how many 'loci' (another name for the location of codons) the cytochrome-c molecule differs from one organism to another. Cytochrome-c is essential for the energy household of a cell, whence it is common to all biological species.

The data are taken from Dayhoff (1972, page D-8). Light gray: small differences. Dark gray: large differences within a species group. Cytochrome-c counts 104 amino-acids and as many "loci" (Latin for "sites"). Bacteria differ about 70% from any other species, and possibly also within themselves. The diagonal always vanishes, as it compares the species' cytochrome-c with itself. The gray-tinted squares show the differences within a group of species.

	Primates			mammals			birds			fish			insects			plants			yeasts		
	h	c	r	h	d	k	p	d	p	t	b	c	f	s	h	c	s	w	y1	y2	y3
human	0																				
chimp	0	0																			
rhesus	1	1	0																		
horse	12	12	10	0																	
dog	11	11	9	6	0																
kangaroo	10	10	11	7	7	0															
penguin	13	13	12	12	10	10	0														
duck	11	11	10	10	8	10	3	0													
pigeon	12	12	11	11	9	11	4	3	0												
tuna	20	20	20	18	17	17	17	16	17	0											
bonito	20	20	20	17	16	17	17	16	17	2	0										
carp	17	17	17	13	11	13	14	13	14	8	7	0									
fruit fly	27	27	26	22	21	24	24	22	23	23	24	21	0								
silkworm	29	29	28	27	23	26	25	25	25	30	31	25	14	0							
hornworm	29	29	28	26	23	26	25	25	24	28	29	24	13	5	0						
castor	37	37	37	40	38	38	40	38	38	42	41	41	41	40	39	0					
sun flower	38	38	38	41	39	39	41	39	39	43	41	41	41	40	40	10	0				
wheat	38	38	38	41	39	42	41	41	41	44	42	42	42	40	38	12	13	0			
yeast 1	46	46	45	46	45	46	45	45	45	43	42	45	43	43	42	45	47	45	0		
yeast 2	41	41	41	40	38	41	40	40	40	42	41	39	38	39	39	43	44	41	23	0	
yeast 3	41	41	41	42	41	42	40	41	41	43	41	42	42	44	42	42	43	42	25	27	0
bacteria	65	65	64	64	65	66	64	64	64	65	64	64	65	65	64	66	67	66	72	67	69

Table 3.2: Comparison of the amino acid sequences
for cytochrome-c

For example, the light gray box of apes shows that their cytochromes are much alike, while the dark grays of the yeasts indicate large differences: they have been changing throughout evolutionary history.

One may look up in the table, for example, that the cytochrome-c protein of dog and horse differs on 6 of the 104 loci. The first rule (genetically similar organisms differ little in behavioral richness) can be seen to apply for the three birds, for example: penguins, ducks and doves differ at most on 4 loci. The second rule (organisms differing much in behavioral richness differ much genetically) is illustrated by all the white blocks: for example, insects and mammals do not differ on less than 21 loci. The third rule (organisms with equal behavioral richness may differ much genetically) applies to all the gray-background blocks: for example, different types of yeast may differ on as much as 27 loci. The table confirms all three above rules: For example, species with hardly any difference in cytochrome-c (like penguin, duck, and pigeon) differ little in behavioral richness; species with a lot of behavioral difference also differ a lot genetically (like the chimpanzee, fruit fly, and yeast); and finally, different yeasts and bacteria differ much genetically.

Dayhoff's atlas further mentions that humans differ on average from other mammals on 10 loci, from reptiles on 14 loci, from amphibians on 18 loci, from fish on 22 loci. These figures agree qualitatively with fossil data, according to which mammals differentiated 100 million years ago; reptiles, dinosaurs, and birds 300 million years ago; amphibians 350 million years ago; and fish 450 million years ago.[33] Quantitative agreement is quite complicated due to the time and locus-dependence of the mutation rates in the genome. The tendency exhibited by cytochrome-c is valid universally. In the preceding sections we also saw two arguments for the machine-like behavior of organisms:

- seemingly conscious behavior like co-operation and self-sacrifice can be understood mechanically, on the basis of the underlying game-theoretical laws, both with and without kinship;
- In all animals, behavioral richness is related to genome as problem-solving capacity to software.

These insights obviously do not explain behavior in nature, but there exists no indication of animal behavior

---

33   Dayhoff 1972, page 48

that is essentially unexplainable in terms of quantitative laws. Rather, it seems there is a lot of evidence that basic behavioral patterns, which to us, humans, remind of altruism, love, kindness, affection, loyalty and so forth, are nothing but the result of "genes fighting for supremacy". In pseudo-scientific words: if a gene propagates efficiently, there will be many of them. This tautology is the first ingredient in our attempt to prove that all behavioral richness of biological species is simply a function of their genes, within a given environment.

3.4 Behavioral patterns

The second ingredient regards the evolution of animal behavior. In the course of time new species arise and others go extinct. For all species along the human genealogical line,[34] a steady increase in richness of behavior is readily observable. For every small step forward in behavioral richness, the genetic program (the genome) needs to be slightly adapted. Bigger steps require bigger changes, and bigger changes require longer

---

34   In *latinomics*: eucaryota, metazoa, eumetazoa, bilateria, coelomata, deuterostomia, chordata, craniata, vertebrata, gnathostomata, osteichthes, sarcopterygii, tetrapoda, amniota, synapsida, therapsida, mammalia, eutheria, primates, catarrhini, hominidae, homo.

programming time, just as in software programming. Although nobody knows at present how these changes were effectuated —how new genes came about— from the analogy with software programming it is evident that entirely new behavioral possibilities require completely different genetic systems.

In this section, I will briefly review some examples of behavioral richness, with a focus on intentionality. The ethological data are taken from a paper by Sverre Sjölander,[35] and from a beautiful book written by David and Ann Premack.[36]

Stereotyped patterns represent the most primitive way in which nature programs motion of animals. They are characterized by the extremely simple relation between circumstances and behavior — so simple that the relation may be condensed in a couple of conditionals: if this happens, do this, else do that. In software language: a single if-then-else loop.

Among the many well-documented examples of stereotyped patterns I mention just two:

---

35   S. Sjölander, On the evolution of reality: some biological prerequisites and evolutionary stages, Journal of Theoretical Biology **187**, 1997, p.595-600

36   D. and A. Premack, *The Mind of an Ape*, Norton, New York, 1983

- Larvae of a dragonfly, Aeschna cyanea, are ambush hunters that camouflage themselves by hiding amidst vegetation. There they wait quietly for a prey to appear.[37] When a larva discovers a prey capable of rapid escape, it pursues the prey with swimming movements, then changes to walking, and finishes with slow creeping movements. If the larva loses visual contact with its would-be prey after having chased it for forty seconds or longer, it performs a three-phased stereotyped pattern: stand still, backward creeping, and pivoting. The function of this pattern is twofold: (i) to stop the larva's unsuccessful attempts to catch a rapidly escaping prey, and (ii) to diminish the probability of future re-encounters with the disappeared prey.

- When a bee has found flowers with plenty of nectar, it takes some of it to the beehive. There the pioneer bee performs the characteristic 'bee dance', consisting of a series of aborted runs toward the flowers. From the details of the dance pattern (dance intensity, dance direction with respect to the sun, run distance, smell of the dancer's body fur) other

---

37   A.S. Etienne, Descriptive and functional analysis of a stereotyped pattern of locomotion after target tracking in a predatory insect, Animal behavior **25**, 1977, p.429-446

bees are able to distil information concerning the location of the newly discovered flowers.

The larva's stereotyped pattern evidently does not require the genetic programming of intentionality. Many animals display the aborted runs of the bee, an example of 'intention movements'. Birds, for example, perform them by crouching low and spreading their wings, as if they were to fly off. That no real intentionality is involved in the case of the bees is evident from the fact that bees also dance when there are no other bees around to watch it. Yet, many handbooks on animal behavior still refer to the bee dance as if it were an example of intentional communication.

Object constancy is acquired by human children of about three years old.[38] Object constancy is the capacity to conceive the identity of an object, even when that object temporarily hides from direct eyesight. Such behavior requires more complicated programming, because a few conditionals (if-then-else loops) will not do. Requisites are memory, and —for computer software standards— quite advanced three-dimensional object recognition. Etienne's larva mentioned above, for example, is able to

---

38   J. Piaget, *The Construction of Reality in the Child*, Basic Books, New York, 1954

anticipate the movement of a prey when it temporarily disappears behind an obstacle (A.S. Etienne, above-quoted article). Such behavior is very difficult to program for humans, but nobody doubts that Artificial Intelligence will someday succeed in doing so. Intentionality does not seem to be required for primitive forms of object constancy, and is not thinkable without it.

The next step in behavioral richness, on our way towards first-degree intentionality, is **serial use of senses**, as particularly apparent from the behavior of reptiles. For example, a snake is able to use different senses in series to catch its prey: that is to say, it is not able to integrate its different senses for a single job. It has to do different parts of the job using the input of a single sense organ at the time. The snake's heat-sensing organs (eyes) govern the striking of the prey. Smell governs chasing the struck prey. Touch finally determines the swallowing of the prey. In all three phases, the snake uses the information of only a single sense at the time! The snake's behavior provides a nice illustration. When a snake hangs from a tree, part of its body coiled around the prey, it searches with its head for the prey by bumping into it repeatedly, until it feels the prey's head. Apparently, the snake is not able to use its eyes for locating the prey's head, although its eyes are available, and open. Clearly, the snake's brain is not able to process data provided by two senses at the time. Since touch best controls the swallowing process, all other senses eclipse at dinnertime.

Birds and mammals realized an evolutionary breakthrough by processing the information of different senses at the time. The biologists in this field call the ability to process sensorial data from different senses, and combine the processed data in the execution of a single act, **intermodality**. From the way in which lions search, hunt, and fight their prey, it is evident that they possess a fantastic capacity of intermodality. Although the associated reality is quite bitter for the prey, filmed sequences are impressive to see, because of the strength and subtlety of athletic performance enabled by intermodality.

First-degree intentionality is the capacity to have intentions. It is not easy to give a full-fledged definition of this capacity. What one needs at least, is two specific patterns of behavior (like whining and eating) which are causally connected (a dog whines in order to manifest a basic need) but not 'mechanically' connected: for example, slavering does not manifest intentionality, since it is directly induced by the sight of food in a hungry subject.

Since intermodal animals are intentional too, it is not easy to find out which of the two capacities came first.

Possibly, they are two faces of the same coin. The behavior of dogs nicely illustrates first-degree intentionality.[39] A dog that has done something forbidden will meet its master in the door, showing clear signs of distress; or, when thirsty, it will push its water cup around until somebody fills it; and when it's time for the daily walk, it will whine and scratch the door until the master makes some signs of getting ready.

Still, the dog's intentionality is very limited. It is able to anticipate only the immediate future. A dog can communicate its anger at the very moment, but it cannot communicate its feelings of yesterday. Nor can it communicate a conditional, like: 'If you punish me for that, I will chew up the carpet'. Some clever dogs may be able to deceive, in order to obtain food or escape punishment, though on a quite modest level as compared to apes.[40] Deception clearly is only possible if the subject conceives that another subject may have intentions. This is the definition of **second-degree intentionality**. Chimpanzees provide convincing examples of second

---

39 S. Sjölander, Some cognitive breakthroughs in the evolution of cognition and consciousness, and their impact on the biology of language, Evolution and Cognition 1, 1995, p. 3-11

40 S. Sjölander, On the evolution of reality: some biological prerequisites and evolutionary stages, Journal of Theoretical Biology **187**, 1997 p. 595-600

degree intentionality. David and Ann Premack showed a chimpanzee a movie of a man jumping for a banana cluster, hanging down from the ceiling. The poor man was not able to reach the bananas. After the movie, the chimpanzee had a look at a set of photographs: one with a man standing on a chair, others with selected items shown in the movie, like the banana cluster itself. In ten of the twelve experiments, the chimpanzee chose the photograph with the man on the chair. This is convincing evidence of the fact that the chimpanzee interprets the man's awkward movements as an attempt to reach for the bananas. It also recognizes the chair as a possible solution to the man's problem. Human children younger than four are normally not able to choose intentionally. They choose associatively instead, for the banana cluster, as it just happened to show up in the movie.

"Behaviorists" deny the existence of intentionality. They surely must have a hard time explaining plenty of empirical data, like the above-mentioned chimpanzee choices. The Premacks are quite unambiguous on the issue of intentionality (see page 50 of their book):

"In contradistinction to this widespread popular use of intention, American psychologists (or at least the behaviorists among them) advise us that intention is not only a vague notion, but a bogus one. There is in fact no such thing as intention, the behaviorist assures us; our belief in it is entirely a self-deception. Quite probably, the behaviorists have fallen into the luxury of self-deception on this issue, confusing laboratories with life. In the laboratory, one can easily dispense with intentions. In testing the human subject, instructions can eliminate lying (since human subjects are inclined to tell the truth), so that we do not have to concern ourselves with intentions. And in testing some animals, starvation substitutes for instructions (eliminating any need to speculate about intentions in these experimental situations). After being deprived of food for twenty-four hours (or being maintained at 80 percent of normal body weight), the pigeon or rat whose food is finally restored is likely to do nothing more than eat heartily."

Second-degree intentionality can give rise to hilarious situations, as in the case of deception among chimpanzees.[41] Clever experiments include teaching a

---

41   G. Woodruff and D. Premack, Internal communication in the
      chimpanzee: the development of deception, Cognition 7, 1979,
      p. 333-362

chimpanzee some specific ritual for obtaining food. When the bell rings, the chimpanzee opens a box, fetches a key and opens the container with food. When a second chimpanzee, who does not know the trick, enters into the scene, a puzzling situation arises for the first chimpanzee. If it simply follows the ritual, it certainly obtains its food, but the second chimpanzee might get to know the trick as well, thereby becoming a potential competitor. So what does it do? When the bell rings, it keeps quiet, as if nothing happened. Only when the second chimpanzee gives up spying, leaving the critical area, will the first chimpanzee approach the box and fetch the key. However, the victim counters this deception: it feigns walking off, but in fact hides, peeking intently from behind a tree. When the first chimpanzee opens the box containing the key, it gives away the secret: a deceiving chimpanzee deceived. An example illustrating the limitation of intentionality among free-ranging chimpanzees concerns the intentional act of pointing (D. and A. Premack, page 56):

"Even though all four young animals developed pointing on a voluntary basis (we did not train them), none has ever used the gesture outside the test space. Even though the animals could have used pointing in numerous situations (to direct buddies to the location of hidden food in the compound, to deceive rivalrous animals, to indicate to their trainers an object or food they wanted), no animal has ever pointed in "free" space. This leads us to conclude that while pointing is not a reflexive behavior, it remains conditioned to the test room; it has not fully undergone the kind of transition that frees it of environmental control. Thus, it has not become a completely spontaneous act that the animal can use, voluntarily, to express its intentions."

Second-degree intentionality requires some degree of abstraction. I have not found a helpful definition of abstraction in the ethological literature, so the reader has to rely on intuition. Abstraction is involved, for example, in interpreting the meaning of a symbol sequence. Chimpanzees are able to associate certain symbols with subjects and with operations. They might understand a sentence stating 'Sarah give apple Mary', meaning that the research fellow (Sarah) is to hand an apple to the chimpanzee (Mary). Chimpanzees are able to understand the convention that the first-mentioned subject is the donor, and the second one receiver. When Mary has had her fill, she is even able to understand the sentence 'Mary give apple Sarah'. These examples show that chimpanzees are able to abstract, in the sense that they can tell the difference between the object and its symbolical function as a pointer toward other objects (or operations). However, chimpanzees do not grasp the essence of syntax: there is no way to tell them the difference between subject and object in a sentence. Without doubt, such a distinction requires a higher level of abstractive power than the above-mentioned one, where the leading position in the word sequence represented the subject.

Two telltale examples illustrating the limitations of chimpanzee abstraction concern map reading and math. Let me quote the Premacks again (pages 103-104 of their book):

> "The ape's failure with normal models, such as photos, television, and dollhouses, had forced us to the extreme of using a model that was identical to the world it represented. Finding that the ape could use an identical room as a model helped us to move toward our ultimate objective — the use of a map. With that in mind, we covered the floor of the model room with a canvas sheet, placing the original furniture upon it exactly as it had been. We next reduced the size of the canvas and the size of the furniture. Then we placed the smaller replicas of the original furniture along the perimeter of the canvas (not the edge of the room), for we were trying to use the canvas as a

representation of the room next door. Much to our pleasure, these reductions and changes, while at first disruptive, did not result in any permanent changes in the animals' performances. They could use the canvas with its reduced furniture as a guide to the real room. We continued to reduce the size of both canvas and furniture until the furniture became no more than a kind of abstract representation of the originals, arranged on an essentially map-sized piece of canvas. While some disturbances again occurred initially, the apes' performances recovered once more. Could we now use the map outside its original room? And if we changed the orientation of the map, could the ape locate itself appropriately? While two of the animals continued able to use the map as a guide when the map was moved out of the room into the hall (a very minor transfer test), all four animals failed to recognize new orientations of the map, even when the map was left in the original room and the angle of change was a mere 45 degrees. So, our elaborate training had really accomplished very little. Not one of the animals could be given the piece of canvas in its home cage (with a mark on one of the pieces of furniture) and then travel the few steps down the hall to the test room and find there the concealed food. Even the two animals that could use the map outside the original model room failed abysmally when shown a new map of another, though familiar, space. The training, for whatever its small success, had failed completely to instill the idea of a map."

And with respect to chimpanzee calculus (page 78):

"Sarah was unable to judge whether two rows of buttons were same or different even before we made any changes in their spacing. Sometimes she judged rows equal or same when they were not, then judged rows unequal or different when they were indeed equal. Since she could not judge number in the initial part of the test, how could she judge any transformations we might make in pressing the rows together or in removing an occasional button on tests?"

As one may readily appreciate, the latter experiment is still miles away from calculating sums and differences. Still, Sarah did not qualify. And Sarah is not just a chimpanzee, but no doubt —after rigorous selection and many years of dedicated training— a very privileged one.

Thanks to the chimpanzees' mastering of the second degree of intentionality, and the corresponding abstraction, their behavioral richness enables many more behavioral patterns than other animals. In a synthetic presentation of chimpanzee observation Whiten and coworkers write:[42]

"Here we present a systematic synthesis of this information from the seven most long-term studies, which together have accumulated 151 years of chimpanzee observation. This comprehensive analysis reveals patterns of variation that are far more extensive than have previously been documented for any animal species except humans. We find that 39 different behavior patterns, including tool usage, grooming and courtship behaviors, are customary or habitual in some communities but are absent in others where ecological explanations have been discounted. Among mammalian and avian species, cultural variation has previously been identified only for single behavior patterns, such as the local dialect of song-birds."

---

42   A. Whiten, J. Goodall, W.C. McGrew, T. Nishida, V. Reynolds, Y. Sugiyama, C.E.G. Tutin, R.W. Wrangham and C. Boesch, Nature **399**, 1999, page 682

They find 39 different behavioral patterns! That is rather poor...

Frans de Waal and Deist or Atheist admirers use such facts to argue that chimpanzees have their own 'culture', in much the same way as also humans have their culture. They normally forget to mention that the chimpanzee populations are genetically much more heterogeneous than human. Woodruff noted this:[43]

"What is often erroneously referred to as "the chimpanzee" comprises at least two well-differentiated allopatric populations that have diverged genetically for more than 1.5 million years. The same heterogeneity is now recognized in "the gorilla" and "the orangutan." There is several times more mitochondrial DNA variation in a single chimpanzee social group than in the entire human species and more sequence variation at chimpanzee nuclear coding (MHC) and noncoding (HOXB6) regions than in humans. It is perhaps more surprising that there is any cultural variation in our own relatively homogeneous

---

43   D.S. Woodruff, *Chimp cultural diversity*, Science **285**, 1999, p.836

species than that there is any in our far more
variable hominoid relatives."

3.5 Intentionality as a measure for intelligence

It is quite impressive that chimpanzees are not able to draw circles, either. Among many thousands of loops drawn by chimpanzees, none had overlapping extremities. These empirical data form the second ingredient of the proof of the incompleteness of biology. In this section the degree of intentionality serves as a measure for behavioral richness, or intelligence. Figure 3.3 shows a species' degree of intentionality as a function of their moment of birth in history. The further subdivision of first-degree intentionality makes use of the behavioral patterns discussed in the previous section.

It took Nature around one billion years, from the birth of planet earth, to create the first cell. It took Nature another billion years to create multicellular organisms. It took Nature another billion years to develop first-degree intentionality. It took Nature the fourth billion years to develop second-degree intentionality. The big interrogative is, how did Nature program infinitely many more degrees of intentionality in only seven million years — those separating chimpanzees from humans?

In spite of the infinite character of the intentional difference between chimpanzees and humans, many biologists keep pointing their microscopes on brain tissue, in search for structural brain differences. A splendid loss of time. So far, the only identified gene that differs between humans and chimpanzees codes for an enzyme that promotes the production of sialic acid:[44] chimpanzees, and all other mammals for that matter, have the gene, while humans do not.[45] Alas for materialism, this brain difference works in the opposite direction. As far as protein expression is concerned, the data are equally deceiving:[46] the differences are negligible with respect to what they are supposed to explain.

For those simpletons who think that brain volume is a relevant measure of mental powers: Einstein's brain weighs 2.75 pounds, a quarter pound less than average.[47] These are the data, and they are definitely stunning. There will certainly be no lack of scientists claiming that third-degree intentionality automatically includes the fourth. What a coincidence, then, that second-degree

---

44   A sugar-like molecule
45   J. Alper, *Sugar separates humans from apes*, Science **291**, 2001, p. 2340
46   D. Normile, Gene expression differs in human and chimp brains, Science **292**, 2001, p. 44-45
47   E.O. Wilson, *Consilience: The Unity of Knowledge*, A.A. Knopf, New York NY, 1998, p. 97

intentionality does not automatically include the third degree! These are non-scientific "ad-hoc" arguments.

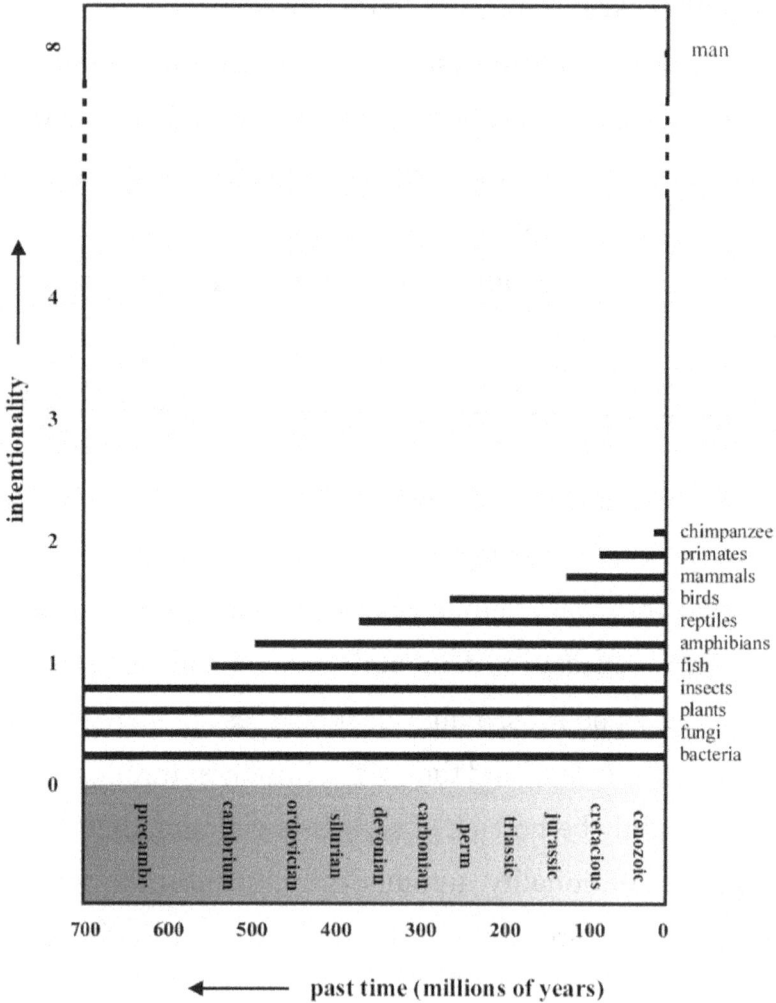

Figure 3.3: Intentionality versus the temporal origin of species.

Consequently, the most reasonable assumption is that the exceptional character of human intentional behavior, and its extremely fast evolution in an environment that was quite similar to that of so many other primate species, is that evolution theory cannot explain high-degree intentionality — that requires spirit, or a *non-material mind*. There you go once again, deism: your fine research helped theism to yet another goal. You can either have continuity in time and evolution, or a Cartesian link between DNA and behavior, but not both together. *If the evolution of humans does not at all fit in either pattern,* then there is necessarily something more to humans than meets the eye.

Yep: 0-3 for theism, because deism dogmatically discards the existence of a non-material mind, and therefore fails to explain Fig. 3.3.

CHAPTER 4

Claim of Fundamental Rights

4.1 Jurists versus Surgeons

Jurists have, mostly unwittingly, a more theist view on human persons than surgeons. The former consider, in their own-made laws, law suits, and verdicts, the human person as being both flesh and mind, although they hardly care about what these concepts mean philosophically, or how they are related.

Surgeons tend to view the human person like all scientists, that is, as a bunch of particles obeying some natural law. But you won't believe your own senses upon witnessing a car crash of a surgeon. Once the surgeon steps out of his or her damaged car, there is no more mention of particles, but only of rights. The Deist still has an escape here, and patiently explain to the dumb Theist that everything that happens after the accident, still obeys natural law (those governing particles). I fully agree. But now let us consider that the surgeon's government decides to split up his family, sell his property to the highest bid, and to put the money in her pockets. Will the surgeon still consider that all that happens is particles moving?

I fear the Deist will. Only a dumb Theist would say: "hey guys, you are transgressing the boundaries of my fundamental rights."

The Deist would rather say, much more reasonably: "F**k off my property NOW, or I will blow your f**kin' head off!" He'd rather die than let some arbitrary nut tread his fundamental rights. Now, my dear surgeon, if you block your Deist preconceptions for a minute, which will be very easy once someone acts toward you without respecting your fundamental rights, then you will suddenly find yourself, just as dumb as before, but a Theist!

4.2 Sharpening Deism's Intellectual Inconsistency

Clearly, Deism has a tough consistency problem here. We can make the inconsistency crueler, of course. Anybody likes Adolf Hitler, among my readers? Well, I had the luck never to know him in person, but I can certify you from his own claims (*Mein Kampf*) and from historic accounts (too many to refer to), that he *would* claim his fundamental rights, were anybody to tread upon them. Now, my dear surgeon, what is the probability that, out of 12 billion different human brains, all would respond equally to a given sound wave? Ask this to your fellow Deist Sir Fred Hoyle, and he would produce you a fantastically small number. A number so small, that one would need trillions of trillions of trillions of universes like ours in order to have a 1% chance to find but a single universe, on which this many-particle miracle occurs.

4.3 Matter is what one sees; does happiness exist?

Thomas Aquinas, an excellent interpreter of theism, declared that human understanding and free will are two properties of a non-material human mind. A mind that God primarily meant to freely communicate with other non-material minds. He never even thought of proving the existence of the human mind, just like our present-day lawyers. In his time, it was not necessary because nobody doubted the existence of the human mind. Today for some professions (lawyers, judges, police, and businessmen) and for all ordinary people (some 11 billion), the existence of a free human mind is obvious, in contrast to nerd professions (physicists, chemists, biologists, neurologists, and neuropsychiatrists). For them the human brain is nothing but a bunch of molecules. How could a bunch of molecules ever 'contain' the human spirit? Indeed, the brain does not 'contain' the human spirit. One could better consider the brain as the communication channel for the spirit. This is the topic of Appendix 2.

I hereby invite the Deist nerd to check whenever animals discussed moral issues, built court houses, or churches. Oh yes, I forgot to mention that chimpanzees do have the impressive number of 39 different behavioral patterns, among which eating, scratching, peeing, and depositing are the four main ones. They can sometimes "behave just like" moral beings, as deists Frans de Waal and Jane Goodall claim. Too bad, these two "scientists" are not even able to distinguish morality (an unobservable property of a free mind) from moral-like behavior (an observable property of animal behavior).

Next, what could ever be the evolutionary advantage of claiming fundamental rights? If there is none, how then is it possible that all human brains agree on one single moral issue, given that morality issues from the brain, and every brain is different? To be sure, there never has been any evolutionary pressure on having certain convictions.

The efficiently self-reproducing brute smashed our cheeks long before we could even utter a claim of fundamental rights.

"Faites vos Jeux", the croupier would say. And all deists put half their fortune on black (animals are moral beings), and half on red (animals are not moral beings). That is the stupidest way to lose all your money in a single night to the casino owner, who took care to put a green zero position on his table.

This was an ever so easy 0-4. Hey coach! Time to replace your complete defense...

Chapter 5

Danish Dishonesty

5.1 This far deism goes in order to kill potential adversaries

Here, "killing" is meant in the reputational sense, not in the literal sense. Yet I believe that in Lomborg's case reputation killing is a far greater sin than ordinary killing, e.g. in a fight between two prisoners. Let me quote Wikipedia, for the worst humiliation deism ever had to go through. Only keep in mind that, as a student, Lomborg was a highly appreciated left-wing AIDS-fighting ecologist, far-better-than-average scientist, who changed insight by careful analysis of his opponents' ideas. He wrote his new insights in a book called "the Skeptical Environmentalist", since its first publication already a *bête noire* of the deist ecological establishment. The following quote is from Wikipedia:

Formal accusations of scientific dishonesty

After the publication of The Skeptical Environmentalist, Lomborg was formally accused of scientific dishonesty by a group of environmental scientists, who brought a total of three complaints against him to the Danish Committees on Scientific Dishonesty (DCSD), a body under Denmark's Ministry of Science, Technology and Innovation (MSTI). Lomborg was asked whether he regarded the book as a "debate" publication, and thereby not under the purview of the DCSD, or as a scientific work; he chose the latter, clearing the way for the inquiry that followed. The charges claimed that The Skeptical Environmentalist contained delibe-rately misleading data and flawed conclusions. Due to the similarity of the complaints, the DCSD decided to proceed on the three cases under one investigation.

In January 2003, the DCSD released a ruling that sent a mixed message, finding the book to be scientifically dishonest through misrepresen-tation of scientific facts, but Lomborg himself not guilty due to his lack of expertise in the fields in question. That February, Lomborg filed a complaint against the decision with the MSTI, which had oversight over the DCSD. In December, 2003, the Ministry annulled the DCSD decision, citing procedural errors, including lack of documentation of errors in the book, and asked the DCSD to re-examine the case. In March 2004, the DCSD formally decided not to act further on the complaints, reasoning that renewed scrutiny would, in all likelihood, result in the same conclusion.

Response of the academic community

The original DCSD decision about Lomborg provoked a petition signed by 287 Danish academics, primarily social scientists, who criticized the DCSD for evaluating the book as a work of science, whereas the petitioners considered it clearly an opinion piece by a non-scientist. The Danish Minister of Science, Technology, and Innovation then asked the Danish Research Agency (DRA) to form an independent working group to review DCSD practices. In response to this, another group of Danish scientists collected over 600 signatures, primarily from the medical and natural sciences community, to support the continued existence of the DCSD and presented their petition to the DRA.

Continued debate and criticism

The rulings of the Danish authorities in 2003–2004 left Lomborg's critics frustrated. Lomborg claimed vindication as a result of MSTI's decision to set aside the original finding of DCSD. The Lomborg Deception, a book by Howard Friel, claims to offer a "careful analysis" of the ways in which Lomborg has "selectively used (and sometimes distorted) the available evidence", and that the sources Lomborg provides in the footnotes do not support —and in some cases are in direct contradiction to— Lomborg's assertions in the text of the book; Lomborg has denied these claims in a public response. Lomborg has provided a 27-page argument-by-argument response. Friel has written a reply to this response, in which he admits two errors, but otherwise in general rejects Lomborg's arguments. A group of scientists, Arthur Rörsch, Thomas Frello, Ray Soper and Adriaan De Lange published an article in 2005 in the Journal of Information Ethics, in which they concluded that most criticism against Lomborg was unjustified, and that the scientific community misused their authority to suppress Lomborg. The claim that the accusations against Lomborg were unjustified was challenged in the next issue of Journal of Information Ethics by Kåre Fog, one of the original plaintiffs. Fog reasserted his contention that, despite the ministry's decision, most of the accusations against Lomborg were valid. He also rejected what he called "the Galileo hypothesis", which he describes as the conception that Lomborg is just a brave young man confronting old-fashioned opposition. Fog and other scientists have continued to criticize Lomborg for what one called "a history of misrepresenting" climate science.

In 2014, the government of Australia offered the University of Western Australia $4 million to establish a "consensus center" with Lomborg as director. The university accepted the offer, setting off a firestorm of opposition from its faculty and students and from climate scientists around the world. In April 2015 the university reversed the decision and rejected the offer. The government continued to seek a sponsor for the proposed institution. On 21 October 2015 the offered funding was withdrawn.

Lomborg's approach evolved in directions more compatible with action to restrain climate change. In April 2015 he gained further attention when he issued a call for all subsidies to be removed from fossil fuels on the basis that "a disproportionate share of the subsidies goes to the middle class and the rich"...making fossil fuel so "inexpensive that consumption increases, thus exacerbating global warming". In publications such as the Wall Street Journal he argued that the most productive use of resources would be a massive increase in funding for research to make renewable energy economically competitive with fossil fuels.

Dear reader: do not be ingenuous. Every move against Lomborg was orchestrated by the EZ mafia. They were just too late to kill him: he was already famous before they even realized his threat. Once a person is universally known, his sudden death would simply be solid proof against EZ. Lomborg is one of those exceptionally few honest atheists or deists, who care more for truth than for their own lives. I would vote him as the best follower of Jesus of the year 2002, even though he is gay (which is no sin in itself) and vegetarian (which is a grave sin against the twelfth commandment, as you might know).

Enough about that silly and sectarian Deism. Time to go to the facts.

5.2 Macrotrends

The Club of Rome, a deist mafia, predicted in 1972 that there would be no more oil in a couple of years. It is only thanks to extreme collective restraint and sometimes, regular war between oil producers, that prices could be kept artificially high.

Figure 5.1 US Crude Oil Prices in dollars per Barrel.

The grey vertical stripes indicate years of economic recession. Until 1970 the crude oil price was about $25 per barrel. Its sudden doubling in the early 70's caused an enormous recession. Its peaking at $120 in the late 70's marked a very short-lived recession. During the longer recession in 1980, the oil price kept falling, until nearly its 1970 level. Apart from the 1989 recession, the oil price stabilized at about $40. During the 2007-2008 recession, the oil price peaked shortly at $160, to fall back, within the recession, to a minimum of $50. The last decade the crude oil price was around $100. Since October 2018 the oil price is in free fall.

The strategy of the oil kings is quite simple. The idea is that, with their huge capital, they buy (in case of "sustainable energy") or discredit (in case of nuclear energy) every possible attempt to generate energy by other means. If a new competitor is growing too fast, the oil mafia just dumps the oil price, until the competitor is as dead as a black hamburger forgotten on the fire. Immediately after the competitor's death, oil prices shoot up again. But not too much... Because the higher it gets, the more money will be invested in alternative sources. In fifty years, there will be as much oil as needed to get the present planet running for 100 years, and yet, it won't be worth a penny.

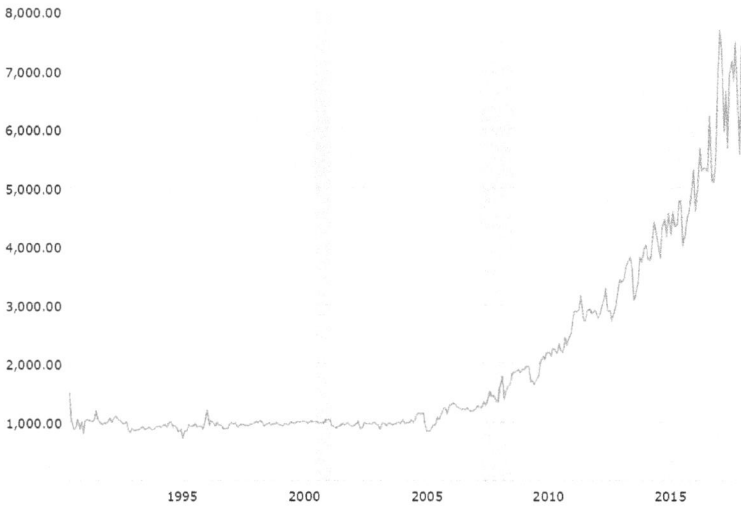

Figure 5.2: US Crude Oil Export (in thousands of barrels per day).

This is the proof that the US do not believe in a long future for oil anymore. They are exponentially selling their reserves. One would only do that if oil is going to lose all its value. The fact that the US's big parasite Goldman Sachs claims that in twenty years the oil price will increase fiercely again, is only a sign that the parasite wants to squeeze the last drops of wanted oil at the highest price possible. This is, by the way, Macro trends' only well-made graph, as it starts out at zero barrels. All other figures have offsets, which is a major sin in science land.

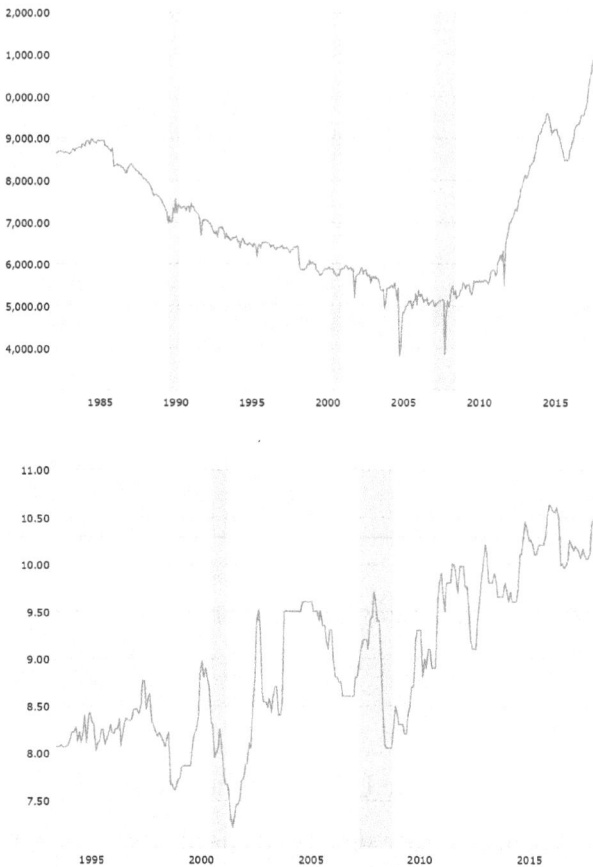

Figure 5.3: US (upper panel) and Saudi Arabia (lower panel) crude oil production in thousands of Barrels per day.

While the Saudi growth rate is 1.5 million barrels every 12 ayears, the US Crude Oil Production has a growth rate of 1.5 million barrels per year. The Saudi's are so dumb as to think this is the right moment to invest in oil refineries. Why didn't they think of it 50 years ago?

Finally, we need the wages. It is already well known that show stars and high directives make an increasingly exorbitant amount of money. These wages double every few years. What would that mean, in colloquial terms? In a non-corrupt market, that simply means that there is an increasing demand for show stars and high directives. It is nothing but the direct application of the offer-versus-demand balance. One might say, nice, that is only for extremely wealthy people. Below we show the British wages since 1855.

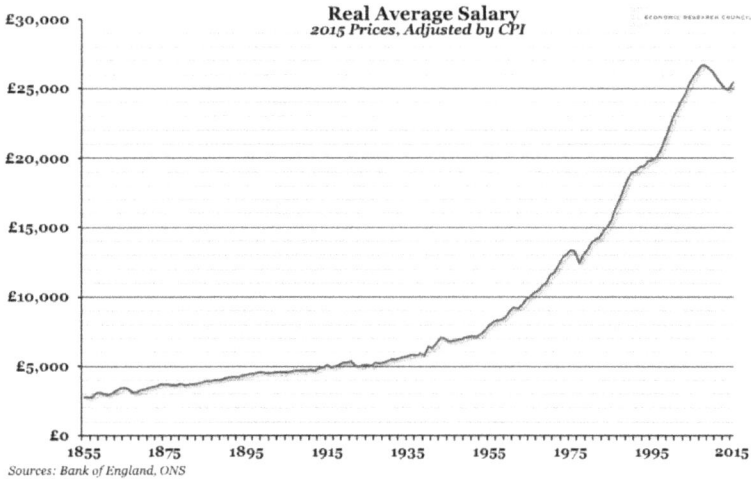

Figure 5.4: Real Average Salary in Great Britain

With a few exceptions, the demand keeps increasing.

5.3 World Population

Fig. 5.5 illustrates both the world population and its growth, both in time and in space.

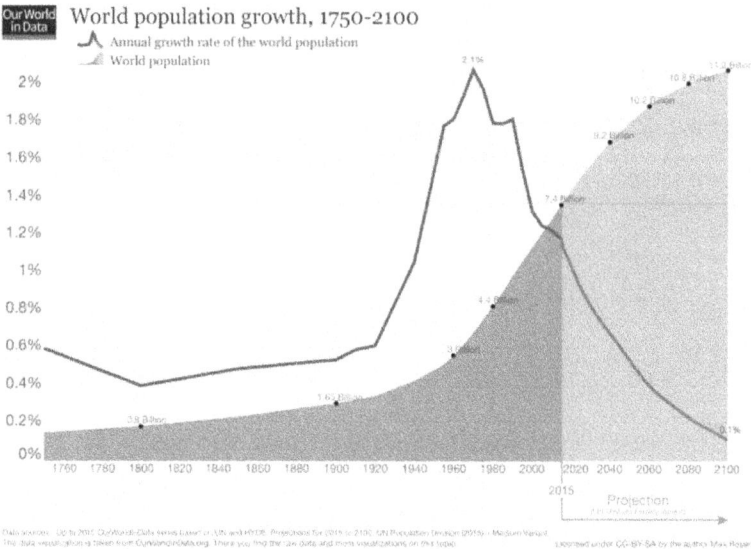

World population growth, 1750-2100

Figure 5.5: Word Population and its Logarithmic Growth Rate in Time

So what do Figs. 5.5 and 5.6 tell us? The wealthiest countries are the orange ones, and they are, in spite of huge immigration numbers in some cases, on the way of genetic extinction. Syria is in red because EZ, the big US parasite, wants Israel to reign the full Middle East. That

Iran still exists is only thanks to Trump, who was so wise as to collectively dismiss his complete EZ-provided body guard, and replace them by his own man. The poor President would not have lived three months, had he chosen to accept the Obama-government's kind offer. The poorest African countries have the highest birth rates. In about 200 years from now, the European gene will have suicided with a huge Darwin Award, as will the Japanese. The majority of the globe is already static. Given the high Latino birth rates in the US, the ex-European genes are disappearing quickly there, too.

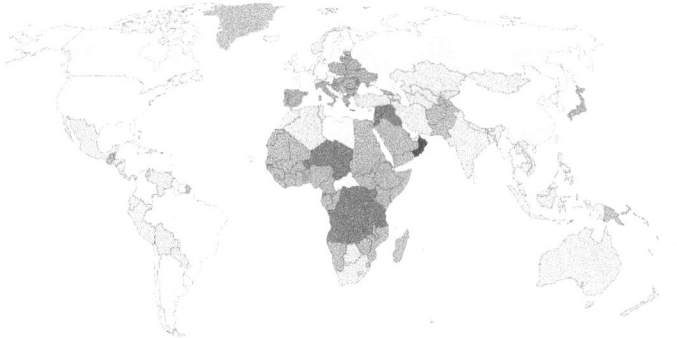

Population growth rate, 2015
Average annual rate of population change (including the UN's 'Medium variant' projections until 2100)

Our World in Data

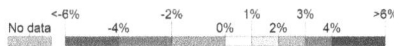

Source: UN Population Division (2017 Revision)   OurWorldInData.org/world-population-growth/ • CC BY-SA

Figure 5.6: Word Population Growth Rate in Space

Clearly, that "dangerous exponential growth in world population" is one big balloon, allegedly invented by club-of-Rome[48] like mafia's, and directly ordered by EZ, the US parasite. Graphs 5.5 show that the world-averaged annual growth rate is, in 2018 (about 1%), already half its maximum value reached in the late 1960's (about 2%). The projection for the year 2100 shows a growth rate of 0.18%, with no sign of saturation. Consequently, the growth rate will become negative in the 22nd century, implying a decreasing world population, and planet earth is never going to make it beyond 13 billion people, no matter how strongly governments promote procreation.

And this while our planet is one big uninhabited desert/jungle! If one erases from the planet surface tiny strips of land bordering big lakes, rivers, or the sea, and one will be left with less than 1% of the population. In other words, world population likes to cluster. Whatever US VIPs said about leaving America when Trump

---

48   What is the fundamental error of the club of Rome? They consider our planet as a single cake to be eaten by all inhabitants — the more people, the smaller one's share. So why do rich countries penalize "agricultural overproduction"! Altogether, humankind weighs less than 0.0000000001% of the mass of the earth. We have still several powers of ten to increase in world population, before that number becomes 1 in ten thousand. With a little more recycling studies, our planet can easily feed a million times more population. Modicae fidei!

threatened to make it to Presidency, they always clung, cling, and will cling together in big, anonymous cities. So they simply stayed were they were.

Normal people usually welcome new lives, and not a single parental gift is comparable for their kid to get to know his or her little sibling. Deists not: they fear or hate the other. "L'enfer, c'est les autres", excellently summarized by Sartre.[49] Why do they fear the others? Well, because most probably they are Deists, too. With Deist ethics.

Deists really have a consistency problem they refuse to delve into. In population matters, it all began with a clown called Malthus. In his "Essay on the Principle of Population" he wrote,

"When there is no obstacle impeding it, the population doubles every 25 years, growing from period to period, in a geometric progression." He also wrote that, "The livelihoods, in its most prosperous circumstances, will not increase faster than an arithmetical progression."

---

49   Hell: that's the others.

Geometric progressions? Arithmetic progressions? What are they exactly, eh, prof. Malthus? Did they follow from some kind of reasoning? Or did these big names just come in handy? Furthermore, on what facts do you base your number 25? Or are you just trying to impress the uneducated?

Poor Malthus gives another turn in his grave.

Yep, 0-5, inevitably...

CHAPTER 6

Quantum Mechanics

6.1 The difference between quantum and classical mechanics

While in classical mechanics a small 3D-system of N particles is described by $9N$ functions of time (3 positions per particle, 3 linear velocities per particle, and 3 rotational velocities per particle), in quantum mechanics the same system is described by a single function of $6N+1$ variables (time, 3 position operators per particle, and three spin operators per particle). Let us make this explicit in the case of 3 particles (A, B, C):

Classical mechanics uses 27 functions of time:

$$\begin{Bmatrix} \mathbf{r}_A(t) \\ \mathbf{v}_A(t) \\ \mathbf{s}_A(t) \end{Bmatrix}, \begin{Bmatrix} \mathbf{r}_B(t) \\ \mathbf{v}_B(t) \\ \mathbf{s}_B(t) \end{Bmatrix}, \begin{Bmatrix} \mathbf{r}_C(t) \\ \mathbf{v}_C(t) \\ \mathbf{s}_C(t) \end{Bmatrix}$$

Quantum mechanics uses one function of 19 variables:

$$\Psi(\mathbf{z}_A, \mathbf{z}_B, \mathbf{z}_C, t)$$

In the function variables of the quantum-mechanical function we use the convention $\mathbf{z}_A \equiv \{\mathbf{r}_A, \sigma_A\}$. Moreover, in both kinds of mechanics we use the convention that, in three dimensions, the bold characters represent three "Cartesian" components. For example, $\mathbf{r}_A \equiv \{x_A, y_A, z_A\}$. Now the reader can answer the fundamental question concerning the difference between quantum and classical mechanics herself: first, the velocity has disappeared in quantum mechanics. For three particles in three dimensions this means a loss of 9 functions of time. From this mere fact one concludes that quantum mechanics can impossibly be deterministic. The second huge difference is that position and spin are degraded, from deterministic functions in classical mechanics, to mere arguments of a function in quantum mechanics. The fundamental difference with the argument time is that the new variables are operators rather than observable quantities, like in CP. From these two fundamental differences one may immediately conclude that quantum mechanics can only predict future *distributions of measureable variables* (position, velocity, spin), and *not* the measurable variables themselves. Using the basis of a "Theory of Everything", one may fill up its space using a 3-dimensional cone:

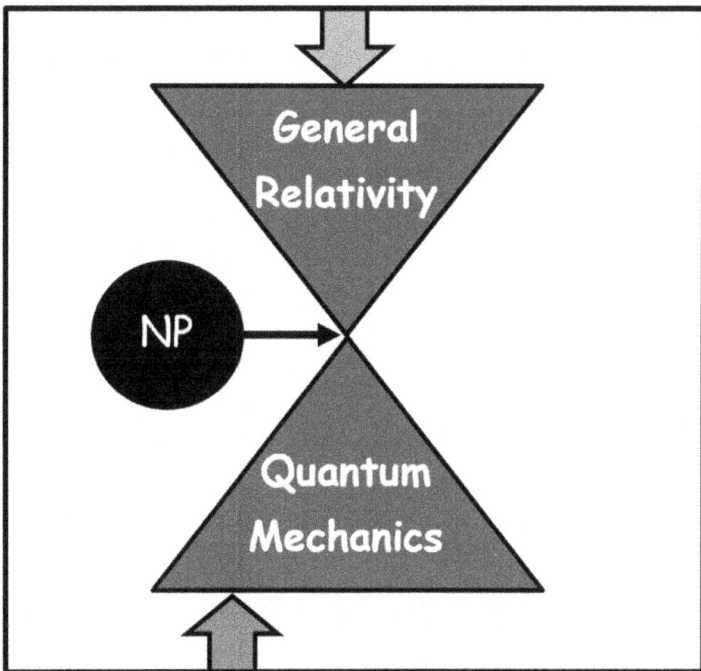

Figure 6.1: A physical domain wherein a theory holds up to a certain degree of accuracy.

The outer rectangle of the "Theory of Everything" represents God's Word through which the universe was created, and which physicists try to unravel. To date, that theory is unknown. Equally unknown are the limits in which quantum mechanics (QM) and general relativity (GR) follow from the Theory of Everything (thick arrows). However, the limiting procedures in which Newtonian physics (NP) follows from either QM or GR are known, and are represented by the singularity of the 3D cone. Since both encompassing theories (QM and GR) hold on the surface of the upside and downside cones, NP holds only on the singularity. This provides an idea of the "volumes of validity" of the three involved theories.

The attentive reader might ask: why switch to quantum mechanics, as classical mechanics allows for full control over all measurable variables? The answer lies in the observations: never has a prediction in the domain of quantum mechanics failed to explain an observation, *even in those cases that classical and quantum predictions were incompatible.*

Hence, concludes the simple-minded philosopher: classical mechanics must be wrong. No sir, classical mechanics are right, in the sense that they give exact predictions in their own domain. Philosophers and philosophizing physicists abound, who have no idea about domains. Their judgments about wrong and right theories are as scientific as are jokes. Yet, even non-physicists can understand the essence of domains. Consider Fig. 2.1. That clearly shows that classical physics holds in a point-like domain with respect to quantum mechanics and general relativity.

In the same way. QM and GR are like point-like domains when considered as limiting theories of an encompassing theory. Nobody knows how many encompassing theories exist between the present level of scientific knowledge and the Theory of Everything.

The other way round, NP seems to vanish in an ultra-small domain. That is not true either, because in nearly all realistic cases NP is far too complex to be calculable, even with the finest computers, and even with the yet non-existent quantum computers. In the limit of reversible processes, for example, statistical mechanics, chaos theory, and thermodynamics play the tiny-dot role in comparison with the huge encompassing NP. Is Chaos theory therefore wrong? No, it is as right as can be, though in its own domain, which is a limit of a limit of a limit of a limit of the Theory of Everything.

This is so simple that a better writer could explain it using but a single page. Yet for deism, such a "limiting absolute truth model" is a curse in Le Comte's positivist church. For theism, it is difficult to grasp, too. Though not a curse in their church.

6.2 Erwin Heisenberg

The three most important discoverers of QM were two
Deists (the Danish physicist Niels Bohr and the German
mathematician Erwin Heisenberg), and an ex-Theist (the
Austrian mathematician Wolfgang Ernst Pauli).[50]
Heisenberg was the first to unify Bohr's series of emission
lines in a single law in matrix mechanics.[51] QM was one
long-lasting nightmare for deism. Nearly every new
discovery needed a deistic correction by Niels Bohr. Up to
date, a serious theist version of the interpretation of QM
has not yet been written. This is due both to the cowardice
of Catholic editors, and to the sectarianism of Deism.

Consider the following thought experiment. In
complete darkness are a single light source and a closed
box with a detector fixed at the back. The detector has only
one special requirement, that it never clicks except when
hit by a photon. The inner surfaces of the box are all

---

50   Pauli often had to reconcile the two Deists, who would not
      speak to one another whenever a conflict arose concerning the
      interpretation of QM.
51   A matrix has a finite number of columns and rows. In order to
      describe continuous spectra (with infinitesimally small energy
      quanta) Heisenberg would have needed infinite matrices,
      which do not exist. This shortcoming was remedied by the
      Austrian physicist Erwin Rudolf Josef Alexander Schrödinger
      in 1926. Present-day non-relativistic QM still uses
      Schrödinger's wave equation and his nomenclature, as do
      relativistic versions.

coated with a 100% absorbing material, such that reflection within the box is impossible. Whenever the detector clicks, one knows with arbitrary precision both the 3D-momentum and position of the photon between the box's entrance and exit, no matter the bloating of Deist Bohr and his flock.

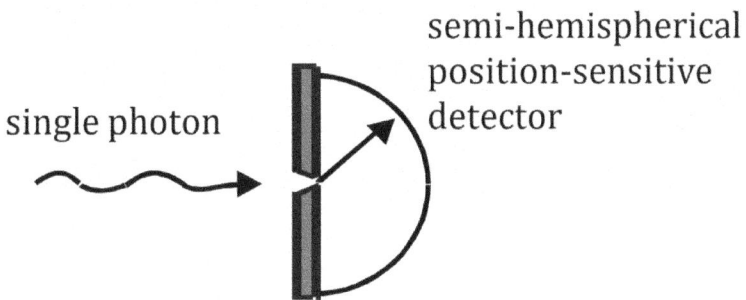

Figure 6.2: The new era of quantum mechanics, or the fundamental loss of full predictive power in physics. A photon in the visible spectrum goes through a small opening (1 micron) to impinge on a detector with excellent spatial resolution. As the errors of measurement of position and velocity of the photon along some axis are linearly related, both can be arbitrarily small.

Heisenberg succeeded in deducing, within his matrix system, the loss of determinism of QM with respect to its encompassed theory, NP. His "principle of uncertainty" claims that one cannot predict both position and momentum[52] of a particle with arbitrary precision. In words: the product of the *predicted* standard deviations[53] is always equal to or larger than Planck's constant (h) divided by 4π.[54] In mathematical scribbles: $\Delta x \Delta p \geq \dfrac{h}{4\pi}$.

This equation literally states that, the better one predicts a particle's position (x), the less one can predict the particle's momentum along the same axis (p). Consequently, if one can predict the position of a particle

---

52   A particle's momentum is the product of its mass and its velocity

53   he standard deviation σ (excuse me, dear reader, that physicists decided to use the same symbol as that of a particle's spin) of a Gaussian distribution

$\rho_{\text{Gauss}}(x \mid \sigma) = N_\sigma \exp[-\tfrac{1}{2}(\dfrac{x}{\sigma})^2]$ is the full width of that distribution taken at 88% of its maximum value, or the half width at 61%.

54   Any quantum operator $\hat{O}$ has a standard deviation ΔO defined by $\Delta O^2 = \overline{O^2} - \overline{O}^2$, where the bar indicates a quantum-mechanical average. In case of the Gaussian distribution of footnote 22, which is centered at zero, the average position $\overline{x} = 0$, because the distribution extends towards negative x-values in exactly the same way as towards positive x-values. Hence, in that special case one may write $\Delta x = +\sqrt{\overline{x^2}}$, where the + choice stresses that a standard deviation cannot be negative by definition (as it is defined as a length of a line).

with arbitrary position (of which we will soon see an example), *one cannot predict its flight direction at all.*

Bohr did not like this literal, scientific, or theist interpretation. Whence he doctored out a clever deistic interpretation: one cannot *measure* the product of position and momentum spread with arbitrary precision. From this sloppy interpretation Bohr further extrapolated an even sloppier one, namely, that a particle cannot have an arbitrarily specific position and momentum at one time. These are two gross interpretation mistakes, which Bohr himself obviously realized: he was too clever a physicist not to understand it. Yet belief was more important to Bohr than the objective truth of scientific interpretation. Fig. 6.2 illustrates Bohr's double mistake.

Consequently, Heisenberg's principle, despite his own claims, is not about the *restriction* of a particle's properties, which are as classical as in NP, but it is only about the *prediction* of a particle's properties. In layman's words: the better one knows a particle's 3D-position, the worse one can predict its flight direction. This does not only hold for a photon, but for atoms, and even complete molecules (as confirmed by many experiments). By simple requirement of consistency of QM, it should also hold for complete planets, stars, and galaxies. So where remains the loss of determinacy of QM (since above we saw that the QM wave function lacks velocity)? Well, that is very intelligently hidden in a combination of Heisenberg's principle of indeterminacy (for a single particle), and for more particles, in the fact that it is impossible to *predict* the 3D-spin (rotation along its own axis) both of the molecule itself and for its constituents. No doubt someone devised, already long ago, an experiment like Fig. 6.2 for spins. If that is true, all those spins can exist and be specific at the same time.

It is funny to note that Heisenberg interpreted his principle of indeterminacy differently, namely, in the context of the "observer effect". According to this effect, it is impossible to observe a natural phenomenon without somehow "disturbing" it. Although some deism-influenced scientists believe in this observer effect, it is clearly established, today, that an interpretation including human consciousness as provoking such a disturbance, is nonsensical. So their cherished example is that of the measurement of a tire's pressure: they claim it as a macroscopic *simile* for Heisenberg's principle. This is so ridiculous that one risks to block his or her jaws from laughter. Their proposal, which imposes an unknown loss of tire pressure, is easily remedied by taking the pains to measure the added volume by the pressure-measuring device. This is common practice in physics since two centuries: the age of Van der Waals' thermodynamics. Of course, they consider the possibility of non-invasive measuring techniques as "not understanding the *simile*". As if their solution to a quantum-measurement problem is the final and only one! Now that my jaws are blocked, I cannot avoid a spasm coming up my belly...

So what is actually left of this deist notion of the "observer effect"? Nothing but the conclusion that humans cannot do what God only can do: know the system from its ultimate causes. Humans are compelled to *observe* in order to gain information of the environment. On the sub-micro-level such observations are exclusively possible using detectors, which, from a mere theist-physical point of view, are nothing but particle absorbers, whether on or off. So what is going on here? Another deist attempt to confuse scientists and laymen.

The worst of all deistic notions introduced into physics by Heisenberg is called the "wave-function collapse". This notion is based on the deistic belief that the domain of physics must be split up into a macro-level (that of human understanding), and a micro-level (that of "clean physics"). Since he felt this notion to be very sloppy, he only mentioned it, and, along with Bohr, preferred to keep it enveloped in mysticism. This mystification illustrates and typifies deism in its true dimension of illogical, anti-scientific sectarianism. Another German mathematical deist, John von

Neumann, tried to formulate a mathematical formalism encompassing both levels (human consciousness, and physics), but his deist ideas were quickly replaced by purely physical ones[55] in the 1980's. Some other deist physicists, like Hugh Everett III, tried to remove the inconsistency of a wave-function collapse by postulating a "many-worlds theory". That is what a sectarian anti-theistic belief like deism ultimately leads to: to postulate an infinity of universes to explain just a single one; which boils down to postulating an infinity of persons to explain just a single one. Although Deists pretend they believe in a creator god, their god is supposed to diminish with every physical discovery.

The founder of Deism, as you might know, is the founder of modern positivism, the French ideologist and pseudo-physicist Auguste Comte. Sadly, for him and his followers, they were later rebuked by their deistic British and German colleagues. Heisenberg distanced himself from positivism:

> The positivists have a simple solution: the world must be divided into that which we can say clearly

---

55   The buzz-word is "quantum decoherence", the scientific term for an approximate inclusion of the immediate environment in the wave function.

and the rest, which we had better pass over in silence. But can anyone conceive of a more pointless philosophy, seeing that what we can say clearly amounts to next to nothing? If we omitted all that is unclear we would probably be left with completely uninteresting and trivial tautologies.[56]

Deists finish by devouring one another. For a healthy Theist, like for a healthy Deist, science is an academic discipline with full autonomy: it determines its own rules, nomenclature, and truthful vision on the materialist dimension of our universe — totally independent of clergy, belief, dogma's and the like. *Theists differ from Deists in that they do not have intra-scientific dogma's.* Healthy Theists might differ in opinion on scientific matters. However, they will never settle a scientific argument by referring to belief or dogma's.

6.3 Dirac's Brackets

The impossibility of predicting observables is a direct consequence of the wave function: she provides a distribution of possible values to measure, instead of a

---

56   Werner Heisenberg in "Physics and Beyond - Encounters and Conversations". New York: Harper and Row

single specific value. This is completely different from classical mechanics and from Einstein's relativity theories. The wave function does not specify the photon's properties, but only what is *predictable* in the photon's properties. This interpretation of quantum mechanics differs from the two main variants discussed at the fifth congress of Solvay in Brussels (1927). On one side, there were the determinists, Einstein and Schrödinger, who were convinced quantum mechanics should be completed (read: restored to determinism) by means of "hidden variables". On the other side the Copenhagen School (Werner Heisenberg, Niels Bohr, and peacemaker Wolfgang Pauli) believed that quantum mechanics needed no mathematical modification or addition. Einstein and Schrödinger lost this battle, mainly due to the very subtle argumentation of Niels Bohr against Einstein's many objections.

Bohr's arguments were so compelling that his victory over Einstein was widely considered as a victory of indeterminist Deism against determinist Deism. Consequently, a world-wide consensus arose concerning Bohr's interpretation of QM. However, Bohr's interpretation of the wave-function collapse kept being a nuisance, because it introduced two levels in physics: the material level, and the level of human knowledge. With time, more and more physicists believe that QM is indeed nondeterministic (sorry, Albert), though that both the wave function collapse and its associated level of human knowledge are extraneous to physics (sorry, Niels). What mainly brought down the wave function collapse was the insight of many physicists that large molecules, and even detectors, obey quantum mechanics in exactly the same way as does a single atom.

More specifically, with reference to Fig. 6.2., it is obviously easier to calculate the experimental outcome by treating the detector as "magic level shifter", as compared to including all atoms making up the detector in an overall wave function. But "easier" in this case means "more approximate". At this moment one can bury the collapse idea as a deist misconception. A full explanation needs some more knowledge of quantum mechanics, which is not so difficult to understand on the level of this booklet.[57]

---

[57]   The fundamental ingredients of a quantum calculation are the initial and final wave functions, which we symbolize as "Dirac-kets" $|\Psi_i\{\hat{O}\}>$ and $|\Psi_f\{\hat{O}\}>$, respectively, as well as the detector wave-function, $|\Psi_d\{\hat{O}\}>$, where $\{\hat{O}\}$ stands for a bunch of relevant operators. In case of a single relevant operator, the relation with ordinary wave functions is $<\hat{x}|\Psi_i(\hat{O})> = \Psi_i(x,\{O\},t)$. That is, an ordinary wave function is a mathematical contraction between a Dirac "bra (<)" and a "ket (>)". The probability of the final function being measured is equal to $P_{df} \equiv |<\Psi_d(\hat{O})|\Psi_f(\hat{O})>|^2$. The final

The quality of the theoretical prediction is not in the purely deterministic propagation, which is calculated either right or wrong, but in the *free human choice* of the initial and final wave functions. Those choices can be more or less intelligent. The initial wave function must be the best approximation of a source-encompassing wave function. The final wave function must be the best approximation of a detector-encompassing wave function. The simplest interpretation of the fact that one may use different-sized wave functions[58] for calculating a single physical process is theist: the choice of the wave functions must be such that the calculation is easiest, without throwing away the baby with the bathwater. However, given that a universe-encompassing wave function exists and propagates, the concept of a wave function *collapse* as a physical process is utterly nonsensical. The only thing that collapses is the approximate wave function. Yet the more encompassing wave function keeps propagating. Of course, also a detector and source-encompassing wave function can collapse. What then keeps propagating is a wave function that includes the whole building, including the people

---

"ket" is nothing but the deterministic propagation of the initial "ket": $|\Psi_f(\hat{O})> = e^{-iH(t_f-t_i)}|\Psi_i(\hat{O})>$.

58   That is, including versus excluding the detector and/or source

inside *as far as biological composites, not as far as intelligent beings.* The most encompassing wave function is that of the whole universe. That wave function is unable to collapse by definition, as there is no external detector to induce its collapse.

6.4 John Stuart Bell

In 1935, Einstein, Podolsky and Rosen published a famous article (called "EPR" after the initials of their authors) on the possibility of a source emitting two correlated particles.[59] They are called "correlated" because whatever spin one measures on one particle, the other necessarily has opposite spin. This is easy to understand in classical terms: the source simply consists of painted particle pairs in which *always* one is blue and the other red. Yet EPR were able to conclude that such

---

59   In terms of Dirac "kets", their wave function would not be an arbitrary (anti-)symmetrized double-argument function like $| \Psi_{general} > \equiv S^{\pm} | \Psi_{1,2} >$, but rather a sum of two products in the form

$$| \Psi_{correlated} > \equiv S^{\pm} |\uparrow> |\downarrow> = 2^{-\frac{1}{2}} \left\{ |\uparrow> |\downarrow> \pm |\downarrow> |\uparrow> \right\},$$ with

$S^{\pm}$ a Pauli symmetrizing operator. The difference between the two expressions is that the wave function of the general expression can be a statistical mixture of pure spin states, while in the second all factors are pure spin states.

correlated sources gave rise to spooky interactions, as they seemed to defy the central pillar of general relativity, namely, that no signal propagates with a velocity higher than that of light in vacuum.

The follow-up of the EPR article had to wait three full decades. John Stuart Bell repeated EPR's calculation, though this time including two polarizers in the set-up. Hence, the display of his results needed an abscissa, representing the angle difference between the two polarizers. His calculation was stunningly universal, not because of the quite basic quantum mechanics, but because he was able to compare his quantum calculations with *all possible classical results*. His 1964 paper demonstrated that whatever classical theory with local hidden variables[60] not only *could not complete the indeterminism of QM*, but *could not even reproduce quantum predictions, no matter how many hidden variables one includes*! The adjective "local" is physical slang for "no information propagates faster than light in vacuum".

Bell's awesome, mind-boggling, horrifying, devastating, terrifying prediction about hidden variable

---

60   A theory with hidden variables" is a deterministic theory with all known variables, and an finite number of possible but unknown variables. The latter are the hidden ones, the former the evident ones.

models for quantum mechanics implied that, if true, it would be inherently impossible to replace quantum mechanics by a determinist theory. Bell's calculation had a huge impact. Physicists from all over the world held their breath. Would Bell's calculation herald the end of determinism, a world view that had allowed so many advances in the past centuries?

A frantic experimental hunt on Bell's theory started. After a few years, it became clear that quantum mechanics described the measured results, *even in those (polarizer setting) regions where deterministic theories with hidden variables failed to do so*, no matter how many hidden variables one wished to include! For a long time, Deism clung to so-called "loopholes", the most important of which the "detection loophole": these are all inconveniences caused by the fact that detectors do not have 100% efficiency. The existence of loopholes did not disqualify hidden variable theories, though at every elimination of some loophole, the hidden-variable theories became more and more fantastic. The last loophole was closed in 2015 by Ronald Hanson, using the spins of two entangled electrons over a distance of 1.3 kilometers.

One of the fossil deterministic Deists is my fellow countryman and Nobel Laureate Gerard 't Hooft. I am not aware of his reaction to Hanson's experiment: this probably means he is not at all interested in the whole discussion of the possibility of nondeterminism. In the year 1932, John von Neumann "surpassed" John Bell, claiming that no kind of hidden variable theories would ever reproduce quantum predictions. Curiously enough, this claim was in plain contradiction with De Broglie's paper of 1927, only five years earlier! How blinded by arrogance should Von Neumann be? John Bell's claim was more modest, as it referred only to the "local" varieties of those theories, meaning that neither particles nor information were allowed to travel faster than light. In 1952 David Bohm published an explicit theory of non-local hidden variables able to reproduce all possible quantum-mechanical results. Looking back on recent history, particularly on deism, John Bell comments, a bit frustrated,

"Bohm explicitly demonstrated how to introduce variables into non-relativist quantum mechanics, whose function was to convert the indeterminate description into a determinist one. More important, in my opinion, it was the elimination of subjectivity from the orthodox version, the necessary reference to the "observer". In addition, the essential idea was one already proposed by De Broglie in 1927, with his idea of the 'pilot wave.' (...) Why did Von Neumann not consider it? More extraordinarily, why did people go on producing "impossibility" proofs after 1952, and as recently as 1978? When even Pauli, Rosenfeld, and Heisenberg could produce no more devastating criticism of Bohm's version than to brand it as 'metaphysical' and 'ideological'?"

In the above quote John Bell complains about the unreasonable stubbornness of deism, represented among others by Von Neumann, Pauli, Rosenfeld, and Heisenberg. In spite of Einstein's loss against Bohr regarding the local-determinist "completability" of QM, I appreciate Einstein much more (leaving apart all his other Nobel-level contributions, which his contemporaries did not value for being too innovative) for considering the concept of "an observer" in QM an altogether idiotic one (see Section 6.3). The consequences of Bell's inequalities are even worse:

all quantum choices necessarily issue from a free agent outside the material universe

For if quantum choices did originate *from within our universe*, then a local hidden variable theory should have been able to reproduce the quantum predictions.

This leads to an overall 0-6 for deism versus theism. Deist dogmatism made this goal possible once again. It's getting boring....

CHAPTER 7

Causality

7.1 Ancient hylemorphism

In material objects Aristotle considered two compositions: matter-form and substance-accident. Examples of the first composition are colorless-eye/color; lengthless-cigarette/length; and marble/form-of-statue.

In all cases, the compositions do not exist as material objects themselves: neither does a colorless eye exist, not does color; neither does a lengthless cigarette exist, nor length; neither does marble exist, nor the form of a statue: *As material objects, that is.* Moreover, Aristotle held the view that the *two member principles are immaterial, and relate like potency to act, while the composition is an existing material object.* Hence, until the very day that biologists achieve resuscitating a mammoth from its presently known shreds of DNA, a mammoth does not classify as a material object, nor does a DNA-designed mammoth qualify as a potential mammoth.

Hence, "actual potency" is the principle representing *any possible actually existing being*, just like "future potency" is the principle representing *any possible being existing* in a given future moment. Hence, "potency" is a time-dependent principle. "Act" is the principle that *actualizes* a potential being, in the sense of bringing it to existence.

A very simple example of Aristotle's act and potency is the following. My actual location is in some office Amsterdam, busily tapping the keys of a laptop. Simplifying a bit, in one minute from now I have but a few potential options. One of them implies no change at all: I did not move an inch. All other options imply a change of location, though subject to Einstein's laws: In one minute from now I cannot possibly be on the moon. Neither could any highly trained astronaut manage such a portent. Hence, potentiality is but an extremely small subdomain of the endless domain of imagination.

The same concepts hold for Aristotle's composition of substance and accident. It is quite more difficult to grasp, and does, in my opinion, add little to the essence of Aristotle's teaching on metaphysical composition, whence I will not discuss the matter in this booklet.

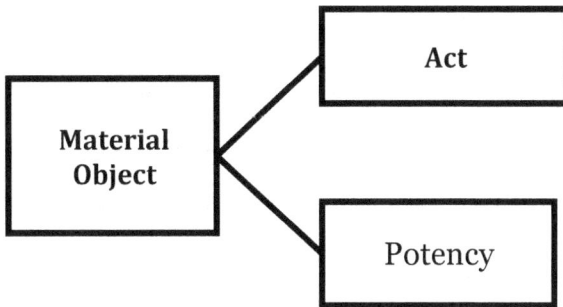

Figure 7.1: Aristotle's metaphysical composition of a material object or being.

The first column represents *a material object or being*; the second one represents *immaterial principles*, both of which are *not* material beings. In Aristotle's view on metaphysical compositions, an object's "being" comes through its act, which is "received" by some potency. The Greek meaning of the Latin-transcribed "hyle" is matter, and of "morph" is form. History gave the name "hylemorphism" to Aristotle's composition of matter and form.

7.2 Thomas' Hylemorphism

Thanks to the writings of Avicenna and Boethius, in the thirteenth century Thomas Aquinas incorporated a second composition into his model, to wit, that of "esse-essentia", or translated "being-essence". These two components again relate to each other as potency to act, and are again both immaterial. At the same time, Thomas holds that the essence of a material entity consists of prime matter and form, which relate again as potency to act.[61] *For this teaching to be consistent, the metaphysical composition of two immaterial members (prime matter and form) can give rise to an equally immaterial principle.*

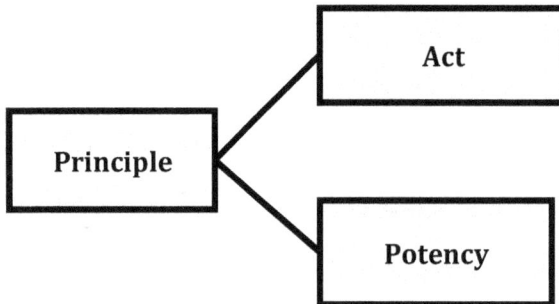

Figure 7.2: Thomas' metaphysical generalization of Aristotle's Hylemorphism

---

61   Thomas Aquinas, Quaestio disputata de spiritualibus creaturis, response to article 1

This is the second greatest metaphysical discovery in history: not only material beings are metaphysical composition of immaterial principles, but an immaterial principle can be such a composition, too! Thomas discovered that an immaterial principle, like the essence of an animal, can be a metaphysical composition of immaterial principles, too.

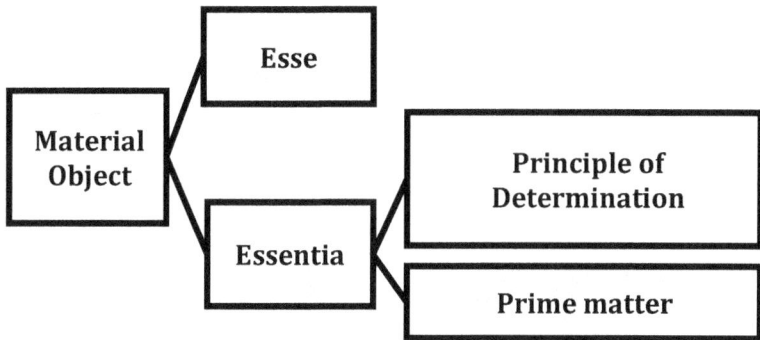

Figure 7.3: Thomas' three-column metaphysical tree.

I do feel sorry for all metaphysicians that the first metaphysical triumph is due to a botanist, and the second one to a theologian. At the same time, I think this very fact points out that, metaphysics cannot be understood unless from a scientific perspective. For this reason, Tomas called metaphysics "ancilla teologiae" (Latin for "theology's maid"). Thomas himself would declare that metaphysics is not a "mere maid", as she not only serves as the dictionary for theology, but she also has the crucial role of providing the foundations for her existence. As natural sciences barely existed in Thomas' century,[62] one can hardly expect Thomas to apply the above ideas to natural sciences. However, once natural sciences had profiled themselves in the works of Galilei and Newton, Thomas' view fitted like a glove to a hand.

All Thomas' intents to keep Aristotle's four different categories of causes (material, formal, effective, and final) alive did not survive scientific scrutiny. This also holds for all other categories of causes,[63] but one: the metaphysical composition of cause into its formal and material components.

7.3 The Failure of Modern Metaphysics

The disaster of 20th century Neo-Thomism is that it completely missed the quantum-mechanical struggle for giving an acceptable interpretation of causality. There are quite some Thomist philosophers who discussed topics

---

62   which was fighting with the definitions of force, momentum, friction, and the like
63   In his "On the Principles of Nature" (Chapters 3 and 4) Thomas Aquinas distinguishes intrinsic and extrinsic causes, causes per accidens and per se, prior and posterior causes, non-coinciding and coinciding causes (like in fire), simple and composite causes, actual and potential causes, and so forth.

like causality, quantum indeterminacy, Thomist contingency, and free will. As explained in the appendix, none of them managed to formulate an acceptable alternative to *the totally unacceptable* interpretation of the so-called "founding fathers" of quantum mechanics: Specifically, Niels Bohr. His nonsensical dogmatic denial of causality in quantum mechanics was happily accepted by the very Catholic philosopher Mariano Artigas and his quasi-school. Too much intent on trying to marry two opposites, he started out with plain contradictions, and was therefore bound to conclude contradictions. For example, Artigas never was able to rationally explain why a human is free to move his hand leftwards or rightwards, whenever he so wishes (in ordinary circumstances). *In order to explain a free human actuation, one has to re-interpret the foundations of quantum mechanics such as to unify (i) causality, (ii) quantum indeterminacy, and (iii) free will, in a single consistent metaphysical theory.*

7.4 Spectrum of Catholic Interpretations

Towards one side of the spectrum is Van Melsen, who rejects any connection between quantum indeterminacy and free will by principle: no discussion possible. At the other end of the spectrum are philosophers like Phillips

(1964), Wallace (1996) or Elders (1997), who do not even mention a possible relation between physical lawfulness and free will. Still others, like Aubert (1965), believe that human liberty has nothing to do with what happens on the infra-atomic level. Surprisingly, Aubert writes that in the inanimate material world causality is inherently deterministic. As mentioned above, Mariano Artigas (1998) stresses the causality inherent in contingent processes, as well as the ontological nature of contingency; he even mentions quantum non-locality and other high-level quantum terminology, but rather stunningly fails to come up with any theistic alternative. That is, he provided a Bohr-inspired deistic account of the quantum measurement problem, *and did not even take the pain to study the relations between the measurement problem and human free will.*

In this respect, Selvaggi (1996) is the happy exception to the rule of large-scale Catholic failure. He recognizes the revolutionary aspect of indeterminacy in quantum mechanics, and states that in quantum mechanics "*the concept of probability is at the very heart of matter, causing the essential indeterminacy in all physical future*". Selvaggi adds that fundamental particles do not choose freely. I fully agree with Selvaggi that it is inappropriate to ascribe free will to elementary particles. Indeed, in a world of only elementary particles there is little fun: everything evolves according to quantum mechanics, and there is nothing more to it, but an angel who chooses what quantum options are realized and what others not. Alas, Selvaggi does not consider thoe agglomerates of fundamental particles that are commonly indicated as humans.

7.5 Proposition for the structure of matter

In this section, I propose a generalization of Thomas' triple-column explanation of a material object or being. This generalization only consists in symmetrizing Thomas' metaphysical structure of a material object.

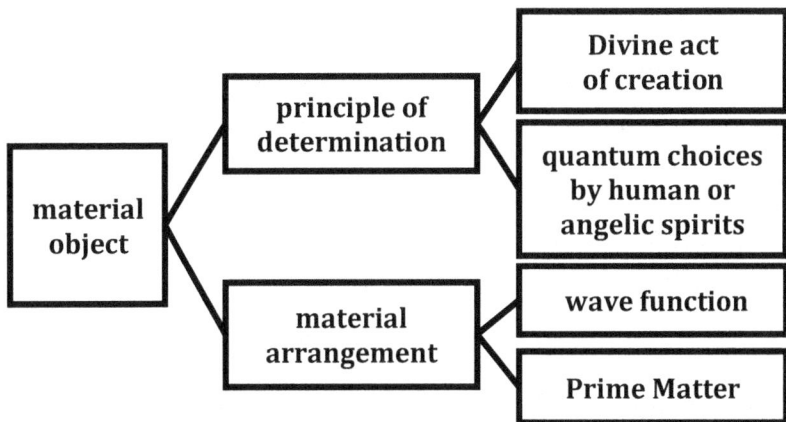

Figure 7.4: The metaphysical structure of all matter called quantum-hylemorphism

As the reader may have noted, the Thomist names for "being" and "essence" have been replaced by "principle of determination" and "material arrangement", respectively. To Fig. 7.5 one may apply, without loss of consistency, Thomas' maxim that *every cause is a principle*.

The "material arrangement" of an experiment, or of a human body, correspond to Thomas' material cause of the material object, while the "principle of determination" to Thomas' formal cause. Likewise, both *causes, which are by definition principles and not material objects*,[64] can be the result of ulterior causes, as pointed out by Thomas.

The material cause of the material object, called "material arrangement" in Fig. 7.5, is on its turn a metaphysical composition of two causes relating to one another like act to potency. These are the wave function and prime matter, respectively. Prime matter is mere potentiality, in the sense of Thomas' doctrine, whence it forms the material cause of the "material arrangement". The formal cause is provided by the initial conditions, and the time-propagated wave function.

On the other hand, the "principle of determination" also is metaphysically composed by two causes, which relate to one another as act to potency. The formal cause

---

64   Bohr's Deistic approach was dogmatically closed to this world view

of the "principle of determination" is the Divine Act by which God gives being to all creatures, and the material cause is a spiritual choice, made by a spiritual being. Apart from miracles God' Ordinary Providence delegates all choices to either angels or humans.

If the material object were a human body, for example, nearly all quantum choices befall the angels: the behavior of all organs. The only quantum choices made by humans are those brain configurations that drive human limbs, eyelids, mouth, lips, vocal chords and breath. Even if the whole brain were needed to determine those quantum choices (which I very much doubt), human quantum choices would still only direct about half a liter of fundamental particles, which is totally negligible with the rest of the human volume, directed by angels.

Hence one should understand by now that the model is fully causal in the sense that when a formal and material couple of causes exists, then so does the effect, *necessarily*. When two effects exist that have reason of a formal–material couple of causes, these two effects *necessarily* cause an ulterior effect. The one big discrepancy with Thomas' view, is that quantum-hylemorphism considers causality as *necessarily* leading to its specific effect, while Thomas considered it possibly leading to its proper effect. That is, causality could fail, according to Thomas. He was not aware that this causal failure would bring down his whole causal system, by introducing an inconsistency in terms: *A cause failing to produce an effect simply is no cause*, however nicely Thomas construes his shop of causality.

Restating the same thing in different words, where with Thomas contingency[65] results as a failure of causality, in quantum hylemorphism contingency results from the human and angelic freedom.

Since God is completely outside his creation, all human and angelic choices are explicit in His Mind before even creating anything. That is, before creating the universe, God already knew the end of it: that is, the individual angels and humans who would make it to heaven, and those who would end up in hell. Theologically, the difference between Catholic and Calvinist predetermination is that Calvinists take human choices to be fully determined by God, while Catholic predetermination is that the Author of true liberty cannot but know what his creatures are going to do with it. In other words, Calvin thought of predetermination as a booklet in which everything was written down. Well, Calvin's booklet has not been found up to date, as far as I know. For Catholics, Calvin's booklet destroys true free

---

65   See the appendix for an explanation of Thomas' self-contradictory view on causality

will. Calvin saw God as a superhuman. That is a huge mistake: God is not a superhuman, but a Being totally beyond human understanding. When God creates free will, He obviously knows what is going to happen with it. Thinking the opposite is inconsistent. *Hence, even though God knows on forehand what everybody is going to do, that does not limit our free will in the least.*

7.6 The Holy Eucharist

Although this does not really add anything to the subject at hand, that is, explaining quantum contingency in a causal way, I will not withhold what quantum-hylemorphic schematic founds the Holy Eucharist.

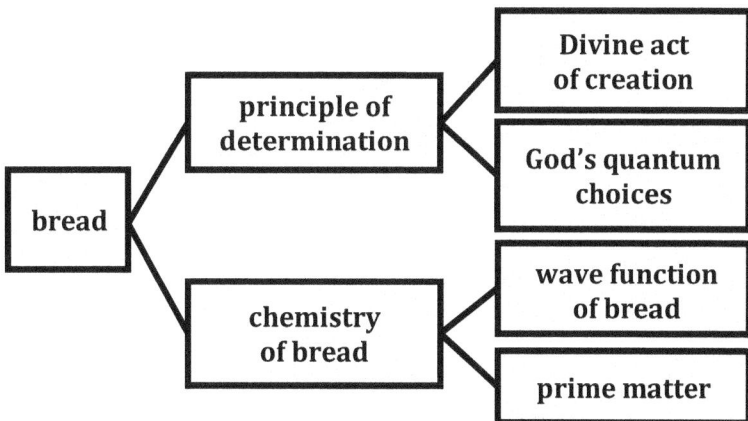

Figure 7.5: Quantum Hylemorphic Schematic of the Holy Eucharist.

In contradistinction, the schematic applying to ordinary, non-consecrated bread should be known by now:

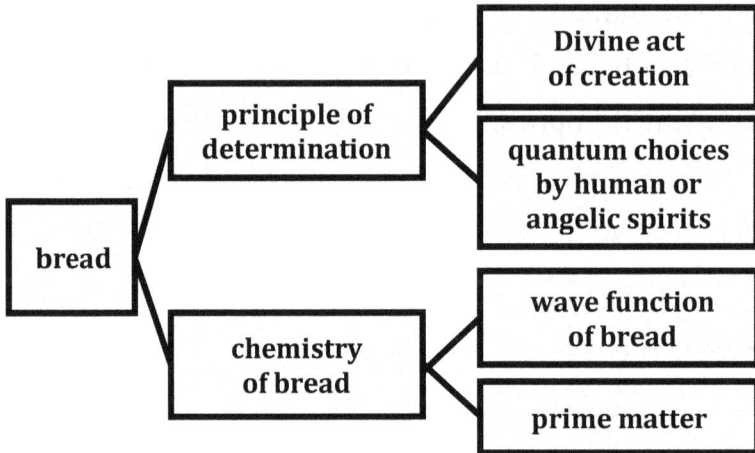

Figure 7.6: The metaphysical structure of ordinary (non-consecrated) bread

One may appreciate, from the above two schematics, that the only difference between ordinary bread and consecrated bread (the Holy Eucharist) is that in the former, all quantum choices are made by angels (corresponding to the microstates of the Holy Eucharist) or by men (corresponding to its consecration and macroscopic location).

With these schematics at hand, Mariano Artigas might open his eyes to the madness of trying to unify two radically incompatible world views. I would add, leave such portents to the politicians. Serious Thomists (how few of them I know of!) would readily understand why this quantum-hylemorphic interpretation of quantum mechanics was unpalatable to Bohr. He would be horrified by the idea that *a single model* can explain (i) Schrödinger's cat, (ii) the measurement problem, (iii) the collapse of the wave function, and worst of all, (iv) the Holy Eucharist.

7.7 Thomas' Failing Causality

For Thomas Aquinas an entity in potency is one that does not actually exist, but can exist, while an entity in act is one that already exists. In Aquinas' own words: "Quoniam quoddam potest esse, licet non sit, quoddam vero jam est: illud quod potest esse et non est, dicitur esse potentia; illud autem quod jam est, dicitur esse actu." To be in act, the being in potency has to receive its actuality from outside, "whatever receives something from another is in potency with respect to it; and the received is its act."

Act and potency are principles, not things. Only when both principles apply together, they give rise to an object, an event, or a particle system. Potency can multiply entities by repeatedly receiving act. Potency determines possibilities yet, in itself, is not able to produce the transition from possibility to reality. The latter is the prerogative of act. To understand the identity of the philosophical and physical causes, it is of great importance to identify "potency" with the totality of possible states, and "act" with a specific selection by a free agent.

Following Aristotle's footsteps, Aquinas identified prime matter with pure potentiality (the absence of any form or determination). We can know or define prime matter only analogically. The Thomist composition of esse and essentia is causal: the "transcendental cause" is the actuality of being (esse), and the predicamental cause is essence (essentia). The causal dimension of being and essence follows from the Thomist assertion that the concepts of "principle" and "cause" are convertible.

Aristotle's hylemorphism was able to explain philosophically the phenomenon of 'change' without loss of identity. Are you the same person after having your hair cut off? Your leg removed? Aristotle's answer would be positive. As we have seen above, according to Aristotle every real thing or phenomenon is philosophically composed of substance and accidents. In case of 'accidental changes' (like the amputation of a leg) the substance remains unchanged, carrying the essence of the person, while some accidents (like the length of leg or arm), which bring the essence to being, are replaced by other ones. An accidental change leaves man man, and animal animal. On the other hand, a 'substantial change' converts a man into a corpse, or wood into ashes.

Thomas' only metaphysical mistake, leading to contradictions in terms in his own theory, consists in his view on "contingency" as a failure of causality. "contingency" signifies that causes may possibly not produce their proper effect. The opposite notion, "causal necessity", signifies that causes necessarily produce their proper effect.

Aristotle did not object to the contingency of final causality. In his discussion of eclipses, he explicitly writes that there is probably no final cause. In his Physics (II, 5-6: 197 a32-198 a13) he explicitly mentions accidental causes, and even 'an infinity of causes'. Aquinas requires causes for all effects; both for the origin of things, and for the permanence of substantial unity. Yet not all principles that can be causes always produce their proper effect: abundant are Aquinas' references to causal contingency. , For Aquinas causes may fail to produce their effect when other causes operate oppositely. Significantly, he founds causal contingency on the contingency of being. According to Aquinas, principle and cause are interchangeable concepts, although the concept of a cause seems to add something to that of principle in its ordinary sense, for whatever is first can be called a principle, whether there results some existence from it or not, but agrees with Aristotle concerning the existence of four causes and three principles, by interpreting that Aristotle's general concept "principle" is here understood restrictively, namely, as internal principles. Hence, Thomas' distinction between three internal causes (formal, material, and efficient) and one external (final) cause, saves Aristotle's inaccuracy (as far as the latter considered the concepts of cause and principle to be interchangeable, too).

In pre-Newtonian science causal contingency was generally acknowledged. Everyone has this experience: even though one pushes a heavy load lying on the ground, it may not move at all, or suddenly move in an unexpected direction. Today such processes are known to be largely deterministic, but not so in the Middle Ages. Hence it is not surprising that Aquinas' concept of cause tends to be blurred by the medieval concept of force. Deplorably, still today many Thomist philosophers confuse the two concepts, leading to a huge pile of junk papers with a strong smell of medieval physics.

CHAPTER 8

Number Theory

This is the most baffling earthquake of all. It's such a pity that, due to the mathematics (number theory), it is not readily accessible. Yet I beg the reader to go through this Chapter at least once, however much you hated mathematics in high school.

8.1 Gödel's Incompleteness Theorem

More than a century ago, the eminent German mathematician David Hilbert formulated the last ten interesting mathematical problems left to humanity. The tenth was the so-called 'Entscheidungsproblem' (decision problem): does an algorithm exist which is able to solve all mathematical problems (of a given kind)? He was convinced that such an algorithm should exist:[66] question was only, the proof of its existence had not yet been found. No wonder he threw a tantrum upon hearing of Gödel's 1930 result.[67] Simplifying a bit, it proved that Hilbert's algorithm *does not exist*. Hilbert's reaction showed that he immediately understood the implications, which so many mathematicians are reluctant to accept: that mathematical truth is a fundamentally superior concept to mathematical deduction. Gödel realized this by demonstrating that

- the consistency of an axiomatic system cannot be deduced from its axioms;
- every consistent axiomatic system always contains a true statement that cannot be derived from the axioms.[68]

In the following, we give an extremely concise proof of the second statement, normally called Gödel's "incomple-

---

66   Remember that for Deists, god is just the mystery guy who made the difference between something and nothing, but for the rest he is not smarter than mathematicians.
67   J.W. Dawson, Logical Dilemmas: The Life and Work of Kurt Gödel, A.K. Peters 1995
68   Kurt Gödel 1930: "Über formal unentscheidbare Sätze der Principia Mathematica und verwandter Systeme I", Monatshefte für Mathematik und Physik **38** p172-198

teness theorem". The theorem focuses on all possible functions of a single argument (a natural number). Consider a matrix R with two entries, the row number and the column number, both natural numbers. *The rows represent all possible functions of one argument, and the columns represent all possible arguments.* According to these definitions, *R[10]* indicates the 10th proposition of a single argument, and *R[10][14]* indicates the proposition obtained when that 10th proposition operates on natural number 14. Gödel's incredible feat of mathematical innovation is his two-stage row ordering prescription: from the row order number a mathematical prescription yields a (much larger) code number, and the code number yields, by a fixed translation prescription, to the symbols making up a mathematical function of one argument. The fact that the row number grows with the length of the code number, Gödel makes sure that his 2D-table contains all possible mathematical statements. Moreover, every row number refers to only one function, and every function refers to only one row number.[69] Next, Gödel defines a

---

69   In mathematics this is called a 'bijection': every element in
      object space is connected to only one element in
      representation space, and the other way round.

subset Q containing only those natural numbers k that satisfy the dot-property (°):

(°) $k \in Q$ ⇔

R[k][k] cannot be derived from the axioms

Since matrix R contains *all possible* statements, there must exist a natural number q, such that *R[q][k]* states that $k \in Q$.[70] The existence of q with the property

(*) $k \in Q$ ⇔

R[q][k] is true

will be indicated with an asterisk (*) in the following. Next Gödel examines the properties of the statement *R[q][q]*, which is known today as the "Gödel number" in mathematical literature:

If *R[q][q]* is false

then (*) $q \notin Q$

---

70   In mathematics the symbol $\in$ is used to signify "is an element of", and when it is barred ($\notin$), it signifies "is not an element of".

then (°) *R[q][q]* can be derived from the axioms
then *R[q][q]* is true

The conclusion being in contradiction with the premise, the latter must be false. Consequently, *R[q][q]* is true. Now let us see what follows from the negation of that false premise:

If *R[q][q]* is true

then (*) $q \in Q$
then (°) *R[q][q]* is not derivable from the axioms
then *R[q][q]* is true

This proves that in a consistent axiomatic system *R[q][q]* is true, but not derivable from the axioms. Since Gödel constructed the true but formally non-derivable proposition *R[q][q]* without a single explicit reference to the axioms themselves, a Gödel truth exists in all possible axiomatic systems.

A typical comment of non-experts is that Gödel's way of reasoning is circular. However, Gödel's argument differs notably from typical circular arguments in that it does not lead to inconsistencies. In footnote 15 of Gödel's article proving the incompleteness of number theory, Gödel anticipated on such criticism:

"In spite of its appearance, such a proposition is not at all circular, because that proposition asserts in first instance the non-provability of a very specific proposition (namely, the q-th diagonal one), and only in second instance (in a certain sense casually) it turns out that this specific proposition coincides with itself." [71]

We now show you Gödel's proof in matrix form:

	1	2	3	4	m<q	q	r>q
1	R_{11}	R_{12}	R_{13}	R_{14}	R_{1m}	R_{1q}	R_{1r}
2	R_{21}	R_{22}	R_{23}	R_{24}	R_{2m}	R_{2q}	R_{2r}
3	R_{31}	R_{32}	R_{33}	R_{34}	R_{3m}	R_{3q}	R_{3r}
4	R_{41}	R_{42}	R_{43}	R_{44}	R_{4m}	R_{4q}	R_{4r}
m<q	R_{m1}	R_{m2}	R_{m3}	R_{m4}	R_{mm}	R_{mq}	R_{mr}
q	R_{q1}	R_{q2}	R_{q3}	R_{q4}	R_{qm}	R_{qq}	R_{qr}
r>q	R_{r1}	R_{r2}	R_{r3}	R_{r4}	R_{rm}	R_{rq}	R_{rr}

71   "Ein solcher Satz hat entgegen dem Anschein nichts Zirkelhaftes an sich, denn er behauptet zunächst die Unbeweisbarkeit einer ganz bestimmten Formel (nämlich der q-ten in der lexikographischen Anordnung bei einer bestimmten Einsetzung), und erst nachträglich (gewissermaßen zufällig) stellt sich heraus, dass diese Formel gerade die ist, in der er selbst ausgedrückt wurde."

Table of Gödel's two-dimensional matrix $R_{row, \, column}$

The matrix element $R_{qm} \equiv R[q][m]$ refers to the q-th function operating on natural number m. R_{qm} is a natural number, too, which is univocally associated with a single mathematical proposition. All possible mathematical propositions are contained in this infinitely large matrix. The line number (first argument) increases down the vertical axis, and the column number (second argument) increases along the horizontal axis. The symbol 'm' stands for whatever natural number. The symbol q stands for a specific number, and r=q+1, is used to keep the table within the page. The arrows all start out from the q-th line and end up at the diagonal. These arrows signify that proposition R[q][m] asserts that R[m][m] is formally undecidable. Since R[q][m] exists for all values of m, it must also exist for m=q. That is to say, R[q][q] exists and it is formally undecidable. Since that is exactly the mathematical proposition that R[q][q] expresses, it must necessarily be true from a meta-mathematical point of view.

8.2 Meta-Mathematics

The last sentence of the first section was what one calls a meta-mathematical expression. It belongs to the metaworld which provides a meaningful ground for mathematics. For example, it is the only way to provide certain insights like "mathematical truth depends by definition on the consistency and meaningfulness of the axioms".

The existence of the Gödel number, its truth and formal undecidability,[72] is not some strange property of only Gödel's axiomatic system, but it is a general property of all axiomatic systems. Gödel himself concludes in his original manuscript: "although the proposition is not provable within the axiomatic system, it has been decided by means of meta-mathematical argument". This only makes sense if truth is a concept of a higher level than formal derivability or computation. It follows that computers can impossibly take over human thinking, because the human mind conceives truth, while computation merely characterizes quantitatively the relation between mathematical tautologies.

The necessary existence, in all consistent axiomatic systems, of true statement that cannot be derived from the axioms, only makes sense if *truth is a concept of a higher level than computation.* It follows that computers

---

[72]   A proposition is "formally undecidable" when it can be proved nor disproved from the axioms.

can impossibly mimic human thinking, with the impossibility degree of mere logic.

The existence of the Gödel number, its truth and formal undecidability,[73] is not some strange property of only Gödel's axiomatic system, but it is a general property of all axiomatic systems. Gödel himself concludes in his original manuscript:

"although the proposition is not provable within the axiomatic system, it has been decided by means of meta-mathematical argument".

Of course, plenty of deistic pygmies contradict Master Gödel, who made school, with geniuses like Alan Turing.[74] That does not refrain me from declaring a 0-7, a singular goal originated from a mid-field keeper's pass, some dribbling, some pirouettes, and a canon shot in the goal's upper left corner. Yep, just like Johan Cruyff in 20th century football.

---

73   A proposition is "formally undecidable" when it can be proved nor disproved from the axioms.
74   Mathematical genius and British savior of millions of lives during WW II, later to be chemically castrated by those very Brits for being homosexual.

CHAPTER 9

Climategate

This Chapter fundamentally differs from all other ones in two aspects: first, it does not discuss a scientific Big Bang; and second, it does not contribute to the score of Deism versus Theism. It is only a sad example of how far Deists are willing to go in order to prove their ideals. The ninth score and Big Bang is the appearance of Jesus Christ on earth, and the prime but silent testimony to His Resurrection: The Holy Shroud of Turin. This topic is covered in some detail in the Appendix.

9.1 The IPCC hoax

The letters IPCC stand for Intergovernmental Panel for Climate Change. It describes itself as "the United Nations body for assessing the science related to climate change". I do not mind about the UN, as everything it does militarily makes me sick. I do mind, as a scientist, that it claims for itself the task of "assessing science" to whatever discipline they fancy. This arrogance makes me puke. Since when does there exist a single scientific luminary in the UN? Who are they to judge scientific quality? They are NOBODY. Scientists are adults, and they are able themselves to assess scientific quality. In doing so, they do not need the assistance of interpol, nor gestapo, nor stasi, nor mossad, nor ipcc. Any interference of these mafias are bound to end up hoaxes. It happened often enough that manipulating scientists were famous for a short time, but were obliged to quit the scientific scene for the rest of their lives: In all continents. and in all disciplines.

9.2 The Hockey Stick Hoax

The hockey-stick data by Mann, Bradley, and Hughes (1999) were meant to scare the public. To my big surprise, Wikipedia forgot to get rid of those data. Remark the noise (the light-grey background) on the graph: the authors did not even bother to decrease it continuously in time, but they chose for three piecewise coefficients. In physical literature, this phenomenon is called "laziness in manipulating data". Spooks like Jan-Hendrik Schön were

unanimously ejected out of the scientific community for
data manipulation.

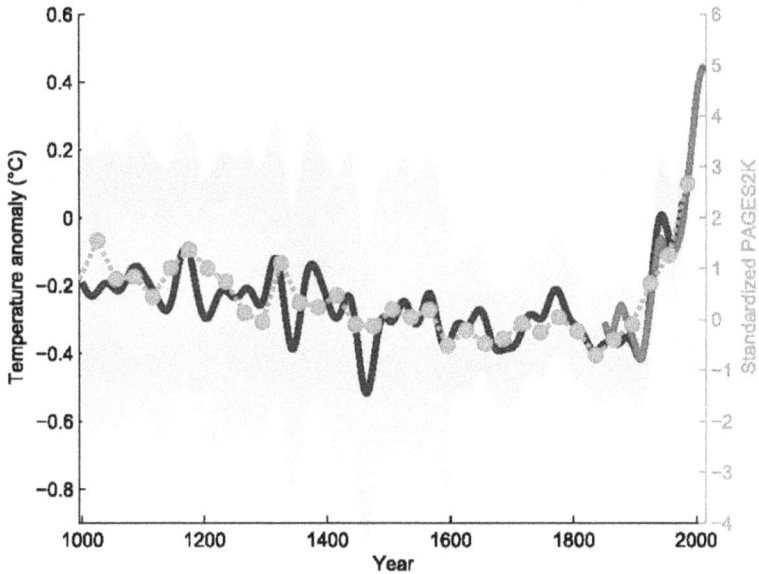

Any physicist can see with a blink of an eye that the above
data set is extremely lousy. For example, the noise bar is
simply a constant temperature offset of 0.4°C from 1000
to 1600. The authors do not mention where that value
comes from.[75] They do not either tell where the sudden
reduction by 50% of the noise in 1600 is due to, and why
it persists until 1940, when the noise suddenly vanishes
during one full year.

---

75   Mann, Michael E.; Bradley, Raymond S.; Hughes, Malcolm K.
      (1999), Geophysical Research Letters, **26** (6): 759–762.

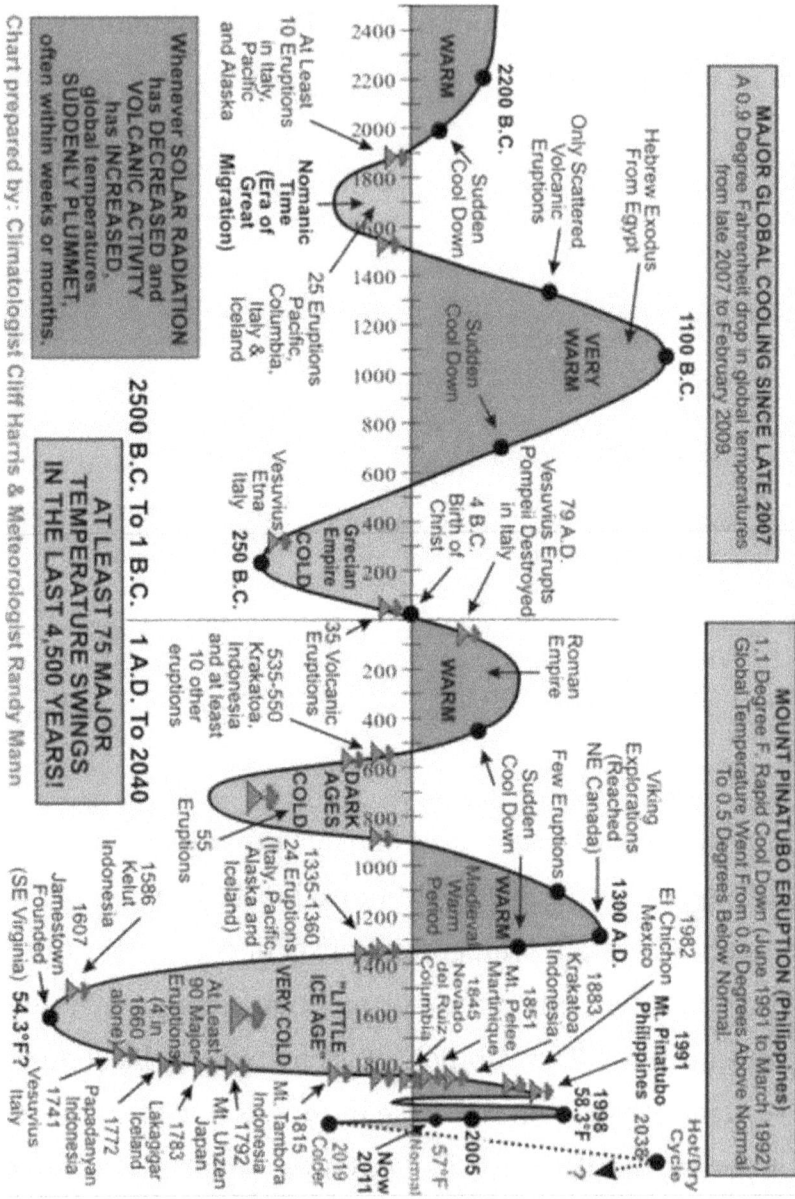

Nearly five millennia of global temperature evolution

The above figure shows how climate effects are primarily determined by solar and volcanic activity. The mysterious but clamorous absent is the greenhouse effect. The more heat emitted by the sun, the more heat collected by its planets. The more dust erupted by volcanoes, the less the solar light can penetrate into the atmosphere. Even a fool can understand that. The recent eruption of Mt. Pinatubo (the Phillipines, 1991) put a sudden halt to the global warming of earth due to increasing solar activity. From 58°F (14.555°C) in the year 1991 the global temperature sunk 1°F (0.555°C) to 57°F (14°C) in 1994, which corresponds to the average global temperature level. In three more years (1997) the temperature suddenly rose to its "normal" (i.e., not polluted by volcanic eruptions) value of 1.3°F (0.7°C) above average. Due to new volcanic eruptions, the global temperature again fell from 1.3°F above average in 1998 to 0.8°F below average in 2019. Nobody can predict the future, *but the scientifically accepted measured data indicate that global temperature has been falling consistently since 1998. In a geological context, this simply means that we are presently heading for an ice age. The glacier lovers can return to building their igloos,*[76] *while the rest of us have to move to warmer areas to harvest our crops.*

Hence, everything said by Al Gore about heating of the earth and the consequential rising of sea levels is straight nonsense. However, Al went much farther than this. *He tried to scare mankind for the earth-heating effect of human activity, and proposed to solve this non-existing problem by dictatorially reducing the world population.* The fact that he succeeded so easily[77] is scaring indeed.

9.3 William Happer

In 2018 physicist William Happer,[78] one of the first physicists to have published on global CO_2 levels, went to a climate conference at UNC-Chapel Hill. On the same day in the morning, he presented a talk specifically meant for an audience of interested laypeople.[79] He started out with some examples of Al Gore's ridiculous scientific incompetence, by pointing out all the physically

---

76   and freeze to death in a fatal substance trip
77   It was EZ that told him to give up Florida, although he had
      regularly won the Presidency against W, and it was the same
      EZ that ordered him to push a suicidal ideology, which can
      only proceed from sick minds as those of the EZ mafia.
78   https://en.wikipedia.org/wiki/William_Happer
79   https://www.youtube.com/watch?v=M8iEEO2UIbA

impossible features that Gore's pundits photo-shopped onto and off an original NASA photograph.

When finished with Al Gore, Happer blamed IPCC for its scientifically nonsensical claims. First of all, on geological time scales the temperature behavior shows not a single abnormality until this very day. The two below graphs, which represent twice the global temperature, though over different ranges of geological time spans, are enough proof of it.

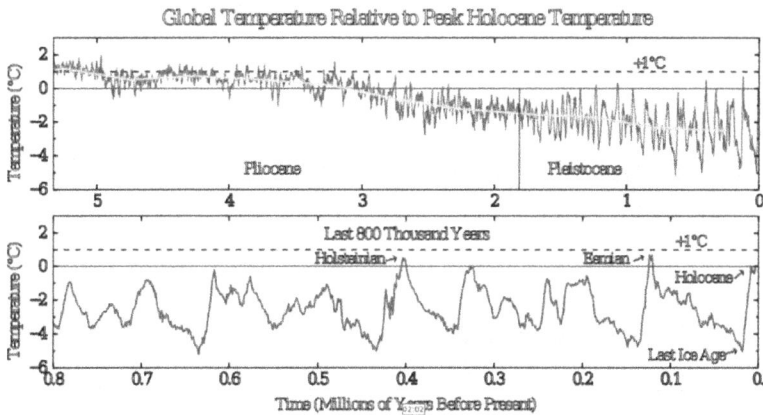

Global Temperatures over the last 800 thousand
(bottom, Pleistocene) and last 5 million years (top).
Apparently, the Holocene is a turning point
in which an on average quickly rising temperature
gives way to a steadily falling temperature.
This indicates we are approaching an ice age
in about 100 thousand years from now.

Greening effect of CO_2 fertilization,
not calculated, but measured. Clearly, green-blue areas
totally dominate yellow-orange-red areas.[80]

Second, Happer pointed out that, for CO_2 concentrations below 150 ppm, plants die. The biological reason is that CO_2 is *not a pollutant, but, together with water, one of the two basic ingredients for plant food.* Without CO_2, no plants, no animals, no humans, no cars, and no oversized Boeings for Al Gore to propagate his nonsense. IPCC presently scares the non-specialists with the claim that the present global CO_2 concentration is 400 ppm, and rising. What IPCC does not mention, however, is that the global CO_2 concentration *never ever* made it below 70% of the present value! Neither does the IPCC mention that the optimum local CO_2 concentration for plants is

---

80   http://russgeorge.net/wp-
      content/uploads/2014/06/Global_greening_map1.png

between 1000 and 2000 ppm; nor that in submarines it is allowed to rise till 5000 ppm, nor that in aircraft till 7000 ppm. These security measures mean that healthy humans easily cope with 20.000 ppm.[81] That is fifty times 400 ppm, by the way.

Global Temperature and Atmospheric CO2 over Geologic Time

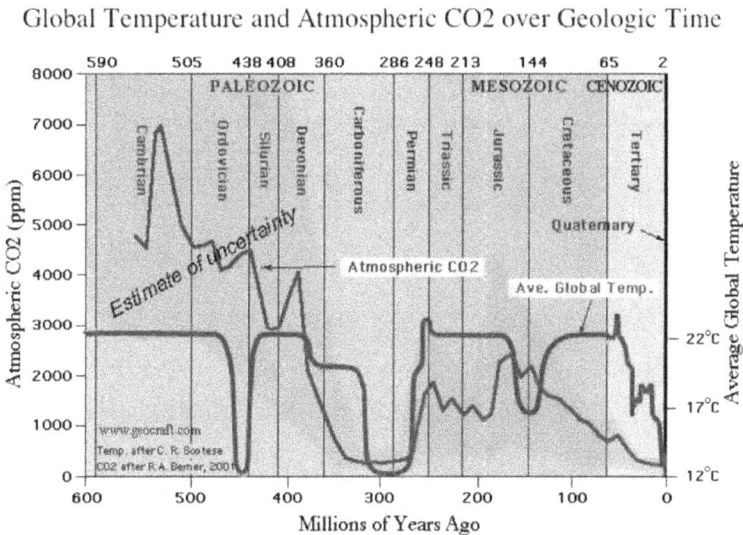

Atmospheric CO₂ and Temperature
since the Paleozoic.[82]

As one may readily appreciate, plants and animals survived the Cambrian atmospheric concentration of 7000 ppm. Not only did biological life *survive* the

---

81   In much the same way, bridges are always designed to stand
      more than twice the officially allowed pressure
82   Data and sources (see lower left corner of the graph) are
      compiled by www.geocraft.com

Cambrian. The latter geological period is also called the "explosion of fossil diversification" by the large majority of paleontologists.[83]

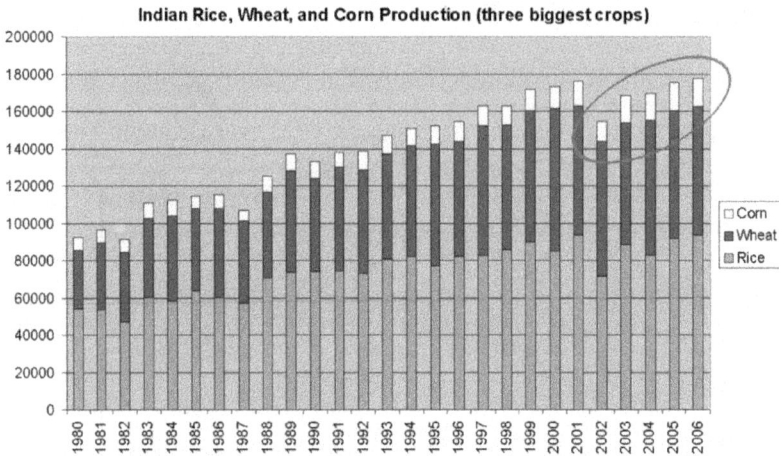

Indian Rice, Wheat, and Corn Production (three biggest crops)

The effect of CO$_2$ fertilization on wheat production

Third, where the infamous and heavily bullied climate scientist Bjørn Lomborg showed that the Kyoto CO$_2$ protocols were at most a splendid loss of money, Happer does not even blink upon stating that these protocols are *harmful* for our planet. As a concrete example of CO$_2$ fertilization Happer shows a graph of wheat production in

---

83   I fear it is not known whether the Cambrian explosion of
      fossils is due to a fossil preservation mechanism (possibly
      related to the atmospheric CO$_2$ concentration) or to an
      explosion in species diversification. In the latter case, one may
      rightfully speak of a "Big Bang" of new species.

India, from the moment that Paul Ehrich published his masterpiece predicting that India would soon die of starvation. I am not able to reproduce his data, although I found the above graph on the web.[84] It shows what CO_2 fertilization is able to do with a country's crop production. From a major wheat importer, India turned itself into a major wheat exporter. Why? *Because they refused to dance the IPCC tango.*

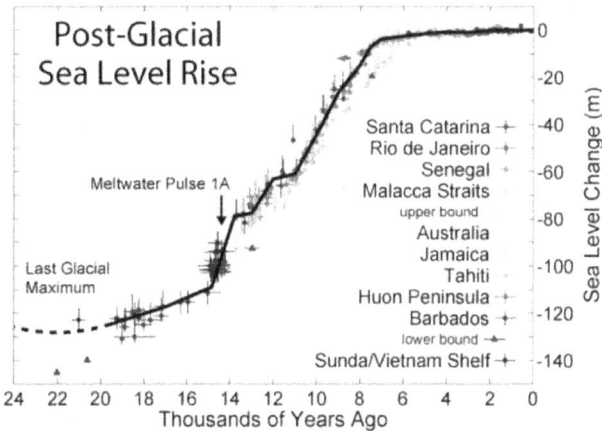

During the last 8000 years the sea level has been roughly constant. During the last ice age, sea levels dropped 140 meter.

Fourth, glaciers started melting a long time before the industrial revolution. Whatever IPCC claims about the melting of glaciers, it is a 100% natural phenomenon that

---

cannot possibly have resulted from human activity. Quite
the opposite: Everything indicates that we are presently at
the very toppling moment of returning to such a
minimum again, rather than witnessing any man-caused
phenomenon.

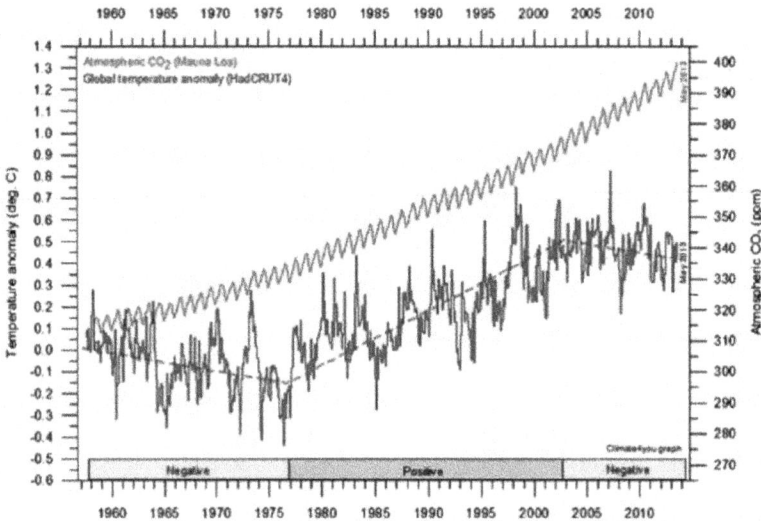

Atmospheric CO_2 and Temperature
over the last 60 years.[85]

However, don't we humans produce tons of atmospheric
CO_2 by combustion? Quite sure we do. But what do
human production rates really mean, when they do not

---

85   theburningplatform.com, which relies on papers like those by
      Ole Humlum, Kjell Stordahl, and Jan-Erik Solheim: Global
      and Planetary Change **100** (2013) 52

amount to more than 0,1% of the rate at which oceans release CO_2 into, or consume CO_2 from the atmosphere? Human intervention, moreover, does not only increase CO_2 levels, but also decreases them, e.g., by extinguishing continental fires. Hence, for all practical purposes, human intervention exerts no measurable influence on the natural ecosystem of our planet, nor shall it ever do.[86]

The oscillations in the increasing CO_2 concentration in the above figure is a summer-winter effect of the Northern Hemisphere.[87] To date it is not known why the CO_2 concentration rises at all. Anyway, over the last 32 years it has risen by 40 ppm. In a geological context, where CO_2 concentrations vary over 5000 ppm, we are talking about a less than 1% ripple on the CO_2 data, and that not at a heat extreme, but halfway an ice age.

Fifth, while the above graph clearly shows that global temperature and atmospheric CO_2 concentration are totally uncorrelated on a 100-year timescale, this does not necessarily mean that they are uncorrelated on longer time scales. The early IPCC claim that on longer time scales, variations in the global CO_2 concentration *precede*

---

86 For scientists already know that the world population is going to decline in about 100 to 200 years from now.

87 The Southern Hemisphere is nearly all oceanic (except Oceania), and therefore lacks the forest-covered area to present a counterweight against the Northern Hemisphere

those in global temperature are full wrong, as shown in the graph below.[88]

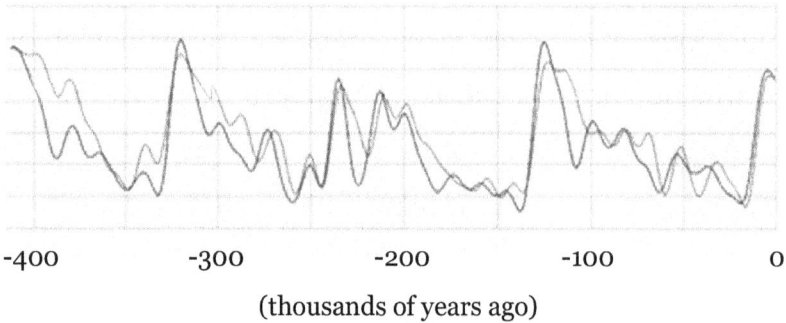

| | | | | |
| -400 | -300 | -200 | -100 | 0 |

(thousands of years ago)

Vostok Ice Core: Atmospheric CO_2 Concentration (Light) Does Not Lead, But Follows the Surface Temperature (Dark) Over a 400.000-Year Time Period

The measured data show that, whether temperature rises or falls, in both cases *the temperature variations lead the CO_2 variations*. Due to reaction kinetics, the CO_2 response to rising temperatures occurs on time scales of hundreds of years, while that to falling temperatures on time scales of 50.000 years. The conclusion is obvious: *IPCC has cause and effect hopelessly mixed up*.[89]

---

88   "History of early polar ice cores", by C.C. Langway jr., *US Army Corps of Engineers*, December 12th 2004
89   With IPCC, this seems rule rather than exception.

APPENDIX

The Holy Shroud

This Appendix describes the second goal of deism. A Theists needs some guts to read it. We are aware of the many excellent books that have been written on the subject. What all these books hint at, due to the fact that the Hoy See did not yet pronounce herself on the veracity of the Holy Shroud,[90] I just write out explicitly, because I consider all proofs water-tight. I do not mean to anticipate

---

90   The Shroud is made of linen and it contains a very special image of Our Lord Jesus Christ. Linen making has been known for the last nine thousand years with Galilee being an important manufacturing center of the cloth. This cloth is also very durable: Egyptian linen wrappings on mummies at least 4000 years old survive to this day, which means the Shroud could have been produced at the time of Christ. The weave is a herringbone pattern with the twist of the yarn being a "z" twist (meaning the spindle was rotated clockwise). The cloth also has a high thread count which produced a fine cloth. Although such cloth was not common, it was not unusual at the time of the Lord especially in the Middle East area. Moreover, cotton fibers particular to the kind of cotton found in Palestine are also present in the linen cloth.

on what the Holy See ever might going to say about it, I simply state my present own ideas about it: without omitting the names of the good, the bad, and the ugly (the trio in the Chapter subtitle).

9.1 Encyclopaedia Britannica

Dear British reader: Your Encyclopaedia celebrates its 250th birthday. Congratulations! Let me introduce the Holy Shroud to you in Britannica's own words:

> The shroud first emerged historically in 1354, when it is recorded in the hands of a famed knight, Geoffroi de Charnay, seigneur de Lirey. In 1389, when it went on exhibition, it was denounced as false by the local bishop of Troyes, who declared it "cunningly painted, the truth being attested by the artist who painted it." The Avignon antipope Clement VII (reigned 1378-94), although he refrained from expressing his opinion on the shroud's authenticity, sanctioned its use as an object of devotion provided that it be exhibited as an "image or representation" of the true shroud. Subsequent popes from Julius II on, however, took its authenticity for granted. In 1453 Geoffroi de Charnay's granddaughter

Marguerite gave the shroud to the house of Savoy at Chambéry, and there it was damaged by fire and water in 1532. It was moved to the new Savoyard capital of Turin in 1578. Ever since, it has been publicly exhibited only rarely, as, in recent times, on the marriage of Prince Umberto (1931) and on the 400th anniversary of its arrival in Turin (1978). In 1998 and 2000 Pope John Paul II arranged for public viewings; he called the shroud "a mirror of the Gospel." Pope Benedict XVI similarly arranged a public display in 2010, and Pope Francis made a pilgrimage to see it in 2015. A replica of the shroud is housed in the Museum of the Shroud in Turin.

Positive **Negative**

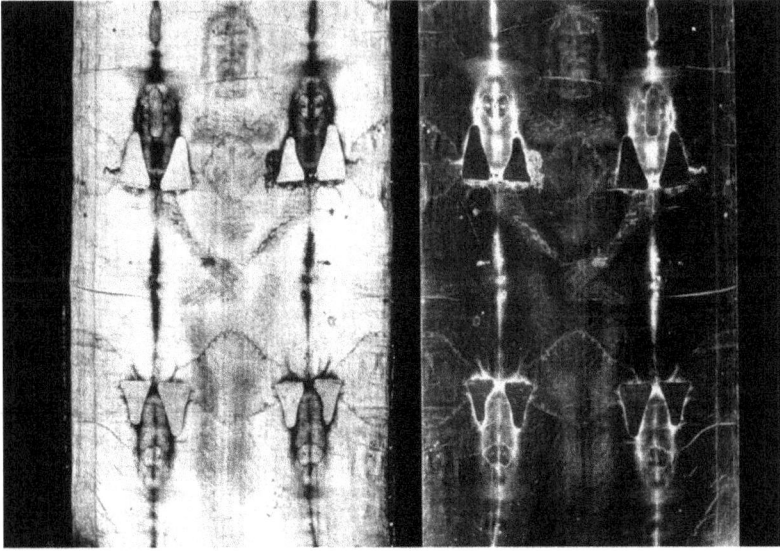

Figure A.1: Upper part of the Shroud of Turin, developed (left panel), and negative (right panel). Head wounds are caused by a crown of thorns. The lower part displays Jesus' back side with over 120 wounds inflicted by systematic flagellation using an especially cruel whip (see Fig. 9.14, right panel).

9.2 Tite's Museum Science

Your Encyclopaedia prefers to use "emergence" instead of "appearance", I know. To appear is the opposite of to disappear, but I have no idea of what the opposite of "to emerge" would be, except for submarines, where it would be "to submerge". Emergence implies some mysticism, or fraudulence. From a scientific perspective, radio-carbon dating[91] is simply a retrograde technique to determine the age of a 600-year old shroud. Just look at the error margin: 130 years are 22% of the shroud's alleged age! Why is the error margin so high? In every other science one only uses techniques of at least one on 10.000 precision. The reason is that the age of whichever measured cloth depends enormously on the amount of

---

91   High up in the earth's atmosphere, where ultraviolet
       dominates (in layers called the stratosphere and troposphere),
       a neutron might collide with a UV-excited mass-14 nitrogen
       atom, and turn it into a negatively charged carbon mass-14
       ion, plus a proton (see the Mendeleev table of elements, in
       Chapter 1), and a high amount of kinetic energy (hidden in the
       velocities with which the two heavy particles move apart). Live
       organic matter uses all carbon available: that is, the highly
       abundant mass-12 carbon, and partially the stratosphere-
       produced and neutralized mass-14 version, fallen to earth, and
       digested by plants and animals. As soon as an organism dies,
       it stops taking in carbon, thereby losing mass-14 carbon to
       mass-14 nitrogen in a spontaneous reaction. The backward
       path is quite different from the forward path, as it does not
       need a UV photon, and occurs by the spontaneous decay of a
       neutron into a proton and an electron. This process has a half-
       life time of 5730 years. Ergo, radio-carbon could eventually
       (not yet in practice, due to technical issues) be the adequate
       technique for dating organic objects that stopped
       interchanging carbon with the environment in a range of years
       from 3000 to 10.000 years old. But dating a 600-year old
       tissue requires a technique based on a physical decay process
       of close to 600 hundred years, which is a factor 10 shorter
       than neutron decay.

radiation it was submitted to. Well, these amounts differ from place to place, and are 100 times bigger than the supposedly linear relation between C14 concentration and time. Now what if the error has been underestimated a factor 10? Then the shroud could have been Aristotle's coat! So let us disregard those carbon data for the time being, as being a typical example of thoroughly bad science, or "museum science", if you wish.

Let us instead have a look at the historical records.

9.3 The Shroud Before 1307

In the "Codex de Pray" (see Fig. A.2 below), one experiences a "close encounter" with the "Mandylion", the classical name for the Holy Shroud of Turin. The above picture shows the burial anointment ceremony of Jesus, as is clearly recognizable from his aura. The picture below shows three possibly weeping women carrying repair tools behind the Mandylion, doubled across its length. The upper side of the Mandylion shows its fabric, in detail, and the circles indicate the places where molten metal drops had fallen on it. The figure on the left might be the local bishop asking the women to repair the damaged parts of the Mandylion.

Figure A.2 "Codex de Pray", late 12th century

First, who inspired the author of the Codex de Pray (National Library of Budapest), written toward the end of the twelfth century, which shows the Mandylion (the medieval name for the shroud) as we see it today, in Turin? Tite's lower bound was AD 1260, which is 70 years after the confection of the Codex de Pray....

Obviously, Tite was not interested in historical proofs. He just received his money to organize the scam, in he did his job quite well.

9.4 History of Christian Iconography

Figure A.3
A 4th Century Roman sculpture representing the Christ: a happy, young, well-built man, beardless, in the full force of his age, and wearing a Roman tunic.

AD 544 Edessa suffered a fierce siege. A heavily raging fire forced the local Christians to retrieve the Mandylion from its hiding place above a gate in their city wall, else the Mandylion would have been consumed by the fire.

Figure A.4: While Edessa is under siege and burning (dark smoke at the top right), sixth century Christians watch as the Mandylion is taken away from its century-old hiding place.

From AD 544 onward, all Christian iconographies came to an instant stall. Throughout Christianity, Christ's iconography changed from whatever local kind into the present known one, that of the sad-looking, bearded man, covered by wounds. As the Mandylion was an obvious danger to Deism, it had to be concealed as soon as possible. For that reason, the hierarchy-mandated icon could not have been made much later, either. *This historical picture on itself already proves the radio-carbon dating results nonsensical.* Indeed, the AD 550 picture, representing Christ's head, is identical to the Mandylion's, down to a submillimeter scale. Even worse for Tite, *this icon dates from 70 years before his lower carbon limit.* According to "Ecclesiastical History", toward then end of the sixth century bishop Evagrius

Scholasticus (536-600) officially declared that the 544 Mandylion of Edessa was "created by God, and not produced by the hands of man" (Acheiropoietos or Αχειροποίητος, literally "not-made-by-hand").

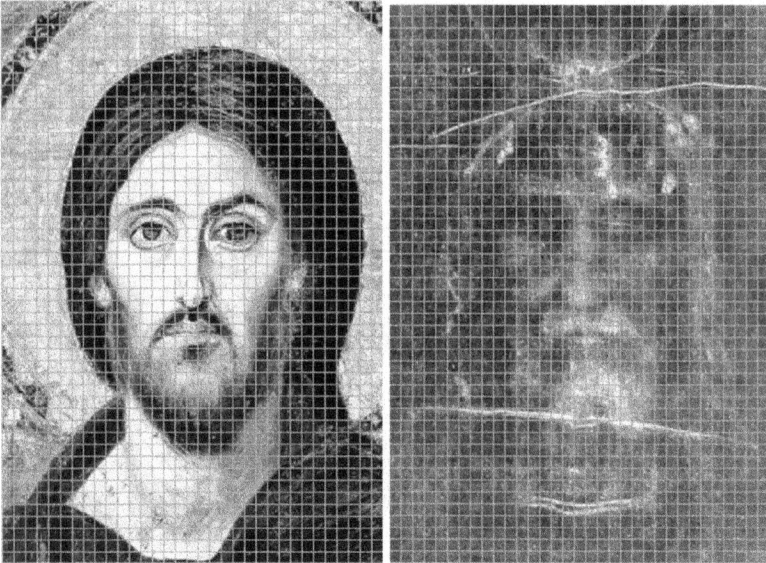

Figure A.5: A Roman-mandated icon of Christ's head from around AD 550 (left panel), and the negative of the Mandylion's corresponding segment. The artist must have had full access to the Mandylion for a substantial period of time.

Again, too bad for Tite, there exists a 10th century picture with Bishop "Abgarus" offering the Mandylion to the faithful for adoration.

Figure A.6: A tenth century icon showing Bishop Abgarus (Evagrius) of Edessa displaying the Mandylion to his faithful.

While Christ's head is quite well reproduced in medieval iconography, a particular detail went totally unnoticed: The nails did not pierce Christ's hands palms, but his wrists. This is very easily recognizable on the Shroud, but the medieval artists missed this detail.

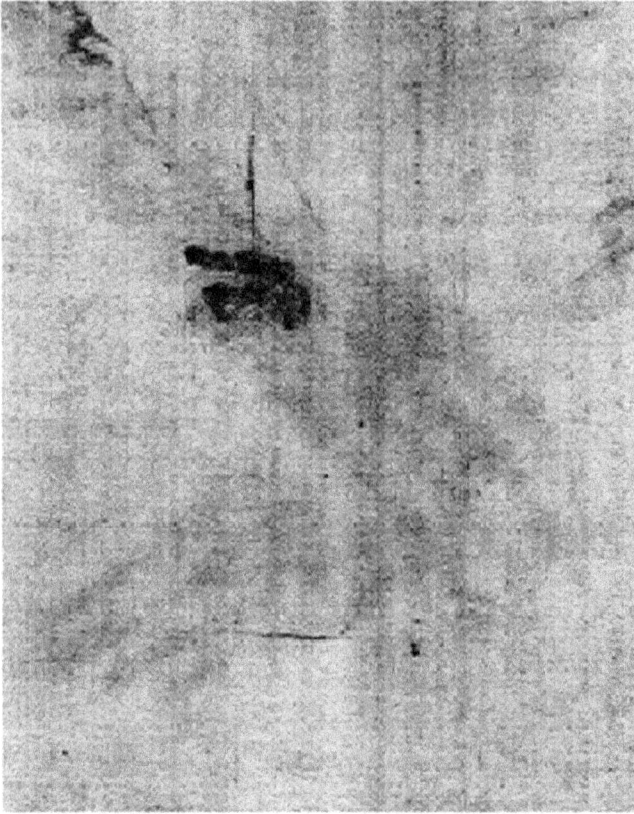

Figure A.7: Not the hand palms, but the wrists were nailed to the cross. Only four fingers are visible on either hand.

Since crucifixion was discontinued after the fall of the Roman Empire, medieval artists did not know that nails through the hand palms would not hold up the human body for more than a minute, as the hands would be torn up by the weight of the body. Neither did the artists realize that only four fingers were visible for every hand. The reason is that the wrist nail destroys a nerve that causes the thumbs to snap into the palm and thus get hidden on the negative, between hand and body. After 554 AD the Mandylion was hidden in Samosata, for nearly 500 years, after which the Knights Templar transferred it to France in several stages around the Mediterranean. Finally, the "Lord's Relic" (the new French name for Edessa's Mandylion) arrived at Paris in 1307. After shorter stances in Lirey and Chambéry, it reached its final destination in 1578 in Turin, as shown below.

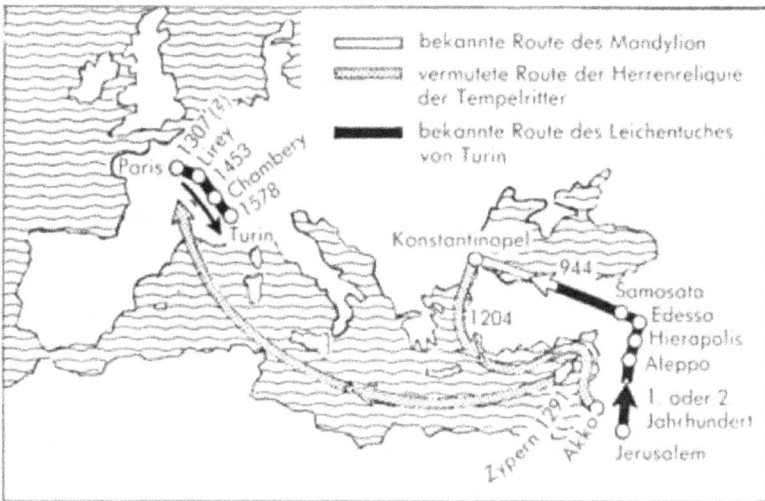

Figure A.8: Itinerary of the Palestinian Mandylion (initial black and white), of the Templars "Lord-Relic" (grey), and of the Holy Shroud of Turin (final black).

Obviously, we speak about the same shroud in all three
phases of its journey through history.

The word of some secret property of the Knights Templar
soon reached the ears of king Philip IV Le Bel of France.
Believing this secret obviously had to be big money, he
had the Grand Master De Molay burnt at the stake in 1314,
as this engraved marble testifies.

Figure A.9: Translation: "At this very place, Jacques de
Molay, the last Grand Master of the Order of the
Temple, was burnt in March 18th, 1314". Jacques de
Molay, was arrested for heresy at the Paris Temple by
king Philip Le Bel of France in 1307. The king
immediately outlawed the Order. De Molay died at the
stake in 1314, the same year in which the king died.

9.5 The French pilgrimage

Upon arrival at Paris, the Knights Templar were very well received by the French "hidden Deist" King, Philippe IV Le Bel, and henceforth designated as Ph-IV. He pretended high admiration for the Knights Templar, while busy with detailing a plan to confiscate all their properties, including the Lord's Relic. Grand Master Jacques de Moley was tortured under the auspices of the Chief Inquisitor of France, William Imbert. In one occasion his arms and legs were nailed to a large wooden door. After the torture de Molay was laid on a piece of cloth on a soft bed. The excess section of the cloth was lifted over his head to cover his front and he was left, perhaps in a coma, for some 30 hours. After seven years of torture by William Imbert, he died at the stake in 1314, after having revoked his torture-forced "heresies". De Molay was the last Grand Master, since Philip-IV had ordered the Military Order to disband. During de Molay's torture, his Knights quickly hid the Relic in Lirey. It took more than a century for the Relic to reappear, in Vignon, in 1453. The Relic's characteristics were the following:

- A square-bottom U between the eyebrows
- A downward pointing triangle or V on the bridge of the nose
- Two wisps of hair down from the hairline in the center of the forehead
- Large owlish eyes, the left one smaller than the right one (viewer's perspective)
- An accent on the left cheek and another on the right cheek somewhat lower
- A forked beard
- An enlarged left nostril
- An accent line below the nose
- A dark line just below the lower lip
- A gap in the beard below the lower lip
- Hair on one side of the head shorter than on the other side

In short: the spitting image of the Mandylion. The Templar's Relic slowly moved southwards, at last appeared in Chambéry, from where it was transferred to Turin. There its name changed for the third time, into the Holy Shroud of Turin. Catholicism is enormously indebted to the Knights Templar for plenty of reasons, mostly for protecting the Holy Shroud during from 1303 through its arrival at Turin.

Figure A.10: A picture of the Vignon Relic, illustrating all the above-mentioned "Vignon markings". The Christ has an expression combining sorrow with a warning pity for the implacable divine justice. That may be the artist's own interpretation, sign of his disgust for the king.

9.6 The 20th century

In 1989 the radiocarbon dating results were published in Nature. Eight years later, fire breaks out in Turin's Guarini Chapel, immediately threatening the Shroud's bulletproof (but not fireproof) display case. Risking his own life among the flames, though "strongly driven by an internal voice", fireman and national hero Mario Trematore used an ordinary sledgehammer to break open the case and save the Shroud.

You naughty Deist: if God does not want the shroud to get lost, you may plan everything you like, but you will never succeed.

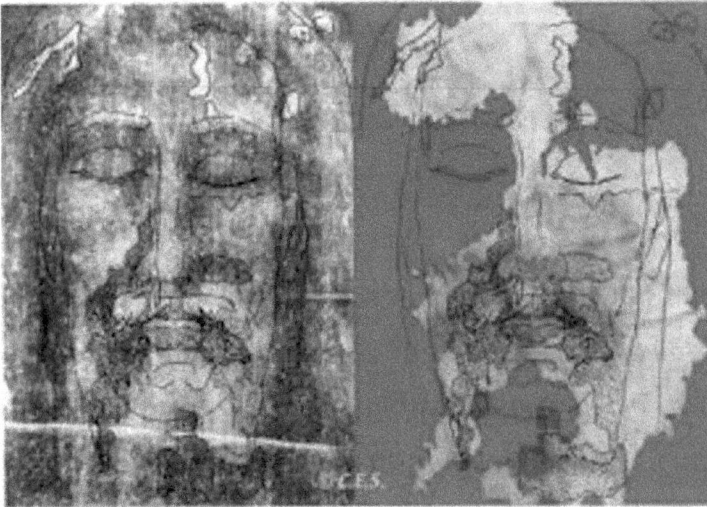

Figure A.11: In 1999 Mark Guscin found AB blood type on the Sudarium (head sweater) of Oviedo. It first appeared there in the eighth century. The blood type coincides with that found on the Holy Shroud. Moreover, the shape of the Sudarium presents perfect overlap with the Christ's face of the Holy Shroud.

The Sudarium is possibly visible in Fig. A.2, too. Tradition, in full agreement with the Gospels, teaches that Veronica used a Sudarium to wipe part of the blood and sweat off Christ's face during his way towards the Calvary, a gesture which He rewarded by leaving his facial imprint on the Sudarium.

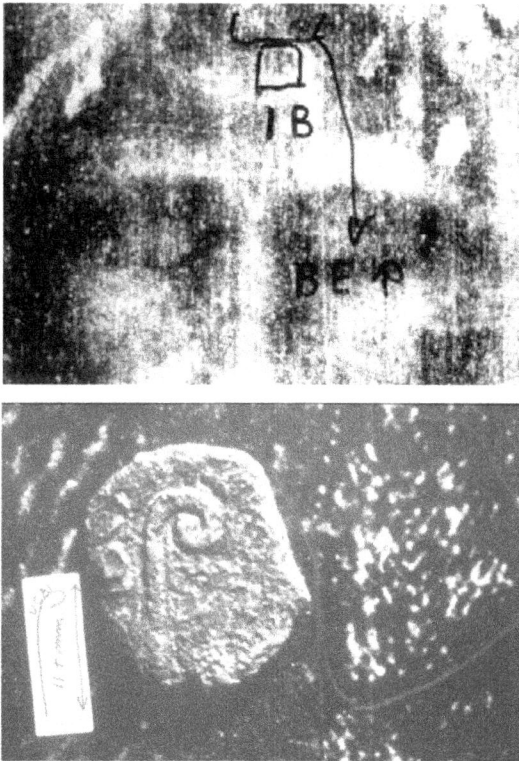

Figure A.12: The miter of Shame

In 1979, Piero Ugolotti reported that he had detected barely visible traces of letters and words in Greek, Latin, and Hebrew near the face on the Shroud, which were corroborated by philologist Aldo Marastoni of the Catholic University of Milan. In 1997, further optical studies were performed by the late Andre Marion, director of the "Institut d'Optique Théorique et Appliquée" and his student Anne Laure Courage. Francis Philas and Mario Moroni identified "U CAI" (left above the staff) as part of the inscription of a lepton coin minted in 29 AD during Pontius Pilate's governorship of Judaea. "U CAI" is possibly part of "TIBEPIOU CAICAPOC" (Tiberius Caesar).

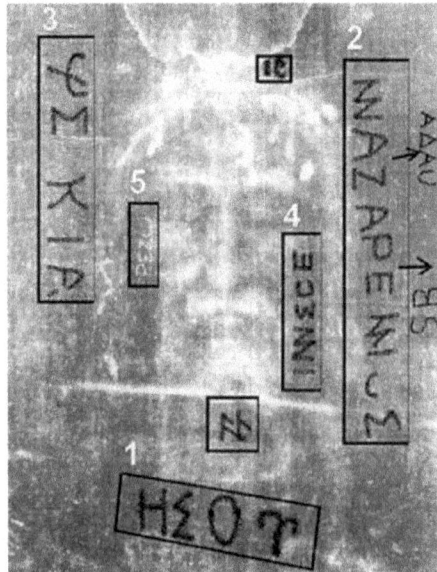

Figure A.13: The ultra-faint texts translated by Barbra Frale

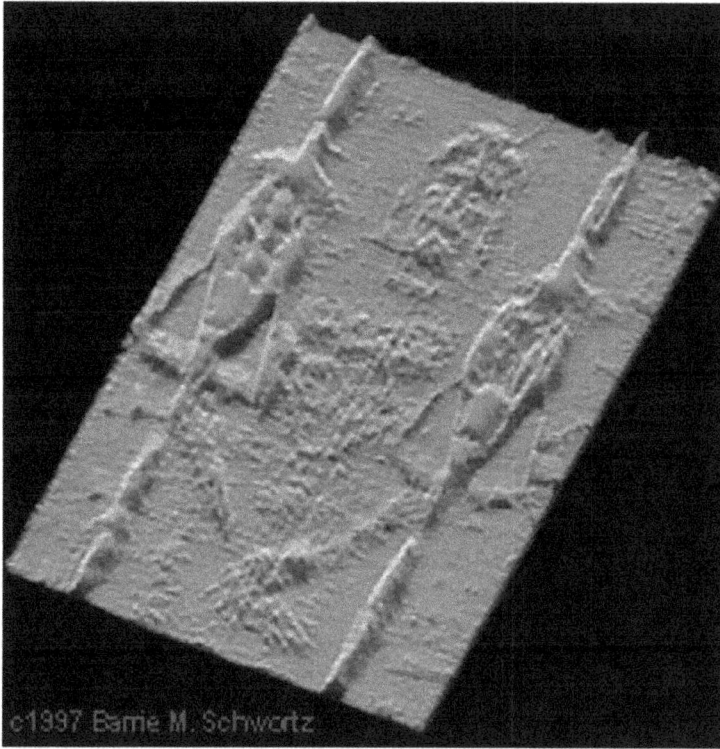

Figure A.14: A 3D darkness-height relationship discovered by Jumper and Jackson, the American founders of STURP. Nobody has been able to explain this remarkable feature.

According to Frale, the letters scattered on the shroud are basically the burial certificate of a man named Yeshua Nazarani. At the time of Christ in a Roman colony such as Palestine, Jewish burial practices established that a body buried after a death sentence could only be returned to the family after having been purified for a year in a common grave. A death certificate stuck to the cloth around the face was therefore mandated for later transfer of the corpse. Taking Marion's texts in Fig. A.13 as her evidence, she concluded that the numbered boxes contain the following terms (full of errors against ancient Greek grammar):

Box	Greek	Latin	English
1	"HSOU"	(y)esu	(J)esus
2	"NNAZAPENNOS"	NNazareNNos	Nazarene
3	"ΨΣ KIA"	(o)pse kia(tho)	taken down in the early evening
4	"INNΣCE"	in nece(m)	to death
5	"PEZω"	Rezo	I execute

Figure A.15: Frale's reconstruction

Putting together these and other text fragments, Frale came to her final reconstruction: "In the year 16 of the reign of the Emperor Tiberius, Jesus Nazarene, taken down in the early evening after having been condemned to death by a Roman judge because he was found guilty by a Hebrew authority, is hereby sent for burial with the obligation of being consigned to his family only after one full year." The certificate ends with a sort of signature: "I execute".

As far as the Fig. A.14 is concerned, the Jumper and Jackson and used a model VP8 darkness-to-height converter. When applied to ordinary grey-scale photographs representing people, VP8 yields laughably distorted and somewhat blurred images: like those one sees of oneself when looking at curved mirrors. Moreover, upon displacing oneself along the direction of the curves (usually upward), the mirror image distorts in a completely different way. An analogous phenomenon occurs with VP8. The role of one's altitude with respect to the mirror curvatures is now played by the position of the light source(s). In case of a single source, posited at the left and illuminating a lying body at grazing incidence, the left part of the model's nose is rendered flat, that is, invisible (because fully illuminated), while the right part of the model's nose is like a huge mountain (because it is in the shadow). In a single sentence: application of VP8 to ordinary black-and-white photographs yields nonsense.

In 1976, a group of scientists at Sandia Laboratories put a 1931 Enrie photograph of the Shroud of Turin into the device and saw what they expected:[92] a truly three-dimensional image of the Christ. This particularly intrigued two of the researchers present at the test, Dr. Eric Jumper and Dr. John Jackson. Stimulated by their startling discovery, they decided to form a research team to investigate what might have formed the image on the cloth and within a few months, the Shroud of Turin Research Project (STURP) was born. Two years later, that same team would perform the first ever, in-depth scientific examination of the Shroud of Turin. Interestingly, only sixty VP-8 Image Analyzers were ever constructed and only two remain functional today. The 3D image shown in Fig. A.14 was made in 1997 by Schwartz and Moran.

---

92   Only image-conversion specialists immediately recognize, from whatever photograph, whether it is going to make sense under VP8 analysis, or not.

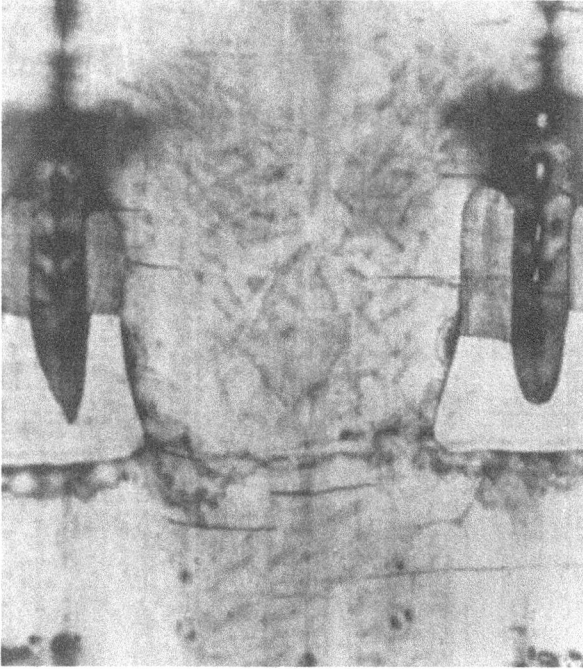

Figure A.16: Christ's back and bottom on the Holy Shroud

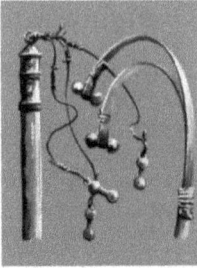

Figure A.17: Artist's impression of the whips used by the Romans

From the angles of attack in Fig. A.16, it seems that Christ was whipped by two men, one taller than the other, who stood on either side of him. The dark, large spots indicate when the halter penetrated Jesus flesh so deeply, that it had to be pulled out by force — exactly as shown in Mel Gibson's master piece "The Passion".[93]

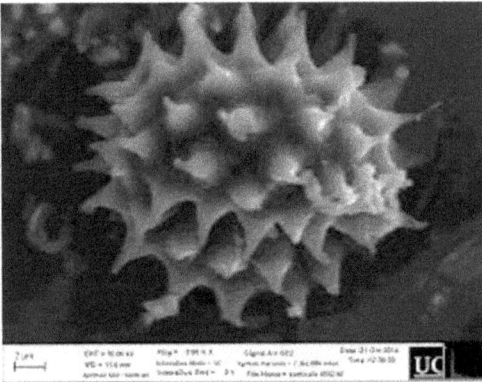

Figure A.18: Image of a pollen (diameter of about 20 micron) found on the Holy Shroud

---

93   Like everybody involved somehow in the Holy Shroud, a special gift from God is granted in the form of great suffering, the clearest example being the last Grand Master of the Order of Knights Templar, Jacques de Molay.

Because of its outer shell (the "exine"), pollen survives tens of thousands of years. Dr. Max Frei[94] found pollen, spores, and molds common to the habitats of the places where the Shroud had been reported. He also found pollen from halophytes, plants typical of the desert regions around the Jordan Valley and adapted to live in the soils with the high salt content found almost exclusively around the Dead Sea area.

In the legend of Fig. A.11, the conformity of Christs' blood type AB on the Sudarium and on the Holy Shroud was mentioned. Concerning Christ's blood, the website of "catholic straight answers"[95] comments the following:

> The blood is definitely human blood. The STURP team determined that the stains were human blood of the AB group. This finding has been corroborated by others: Professor Pierluigi Baima Bollone, Professor of Medicine at the University of Turin, reported in 1978 that the blood stains were indeed human blood with traces of aloes and myrrh and belonging to the group AB. French geneticist Professor Jerome Lejeune also

94   Professor of the University of Zurich, and founder of the Zurich Criminal Police's Scientific Service
95   http://catholicstraightanswers.com/what-is-the-shroud-of-turin/

concluded that the blood sample he obtained was human hemoglobin.

Another intriguing point is that the blood marks on the Shroud are clear and red, not dark brown as typical of dried blood. Also the blood stains are complete without signs of flaking off. Dr. Gilbert Lavoie suggested that what appears on the Shroud is more an exudate from clotted wounds rather than whole blood. Likewise, Dr. Alan Adler explained that the torture, scourging, and crucifixion suffered by the man produced a hemolysis (break-up of red blood corpuscles), which would produce the lasting red color of the exudate.

No pigments, paints, dyes, or stains have been found in the fibrils. X-ray fluorescence and microchemistry on the fibrils eliminate the possibility of paint being used as a method of creating the image, and ultraviolet and infrared evaluation have confirmed these studies. If paint had been used, it would have penetrated through the top fibers onto the lower fibers in the herringbone weave; however, the image is only on the top fibers with the lower fibers being untouched. Also, the image was resistant to bleaching and other standard chemical agents that would have reacted with paint or some other medium. [...]

The photographs of the Shroud also seem to be like X-rays with the images of bones visible. Dr. Michael Blunt, Challis Professor of Anatomy at the University of Sydney, noted that in the hands one can see metacarpal bones and three phalange bones of each finger. Professor Alan Whanger of Duke University noted that the skull is visible.

Dr. Gilbert Lavoie in his recent work, *Unlocking the Secrets of the Shroud*, presented another intriguing discovery. The negative image of the Shroud as compared with the negative images of photography reveals that the man in question had either white or light blond hair. He noted another peculiarity: the shadows of the face and the fall of the hair indicate that the man was upright and suspended when the image was made, while the blood marks indicate the man was in the supine position on top of the cloth with the rest folded over him. Dr. Lavoie concluded that this upright image was made after the blood had stained the cloth: "This finding is intellectually exciting to anyone who contemplates the possibility that this image reflects the moment of the resurrection" [...].

Interestingly too, that where the blood stains appear, there is no image underneath on the fibrils, suggesting that the image had been made *after* the blood stains; obviously, an artist would have worked in reverse, painting the image and then applying the blood stains. Finally, no Medieval artist had the skill to paint a negative image or the perfection of the image with such subtle coloration.

How then was the image made if it was not painted? [...] The image is a surface image, affecting the topmost fibers only without any apparent penetration to any depth (again disproving the "painting" theory). The image seems almost like a big scorch mark, like the scorch marks left from an iron. Also, the fibers on the image appear older and degraded when compared with the fibers outside the image, as though something were taken away from them rather than added, like paint. Yet, the fibers of the image are different from scorch fibers: ultraviolet fluorescence photography revealed that the body image does not fluoresce red when irradiated with ultraviolet light, whereas the scorched areas caused by the fire of 1532 do. Some of the scientists, therefore, posited that a type a thermo-nuclear reaction occurred which caused the image on the Shroud. Actually, when one thinks of Jesus rising body and soul from the dead in a radically transformed existence, such a scientific theory is intriguing.

9.7 The stupids, the bad, and the ugly

Until now this looks like an eighth goal for Theism. However, the bad (Tite) and the ugly (Ballestrero) managed to turn a full-fledged theistic victory in a bitter loss. The quote continues with this hammer blow:

> The most critical controversy surrounds the carbon dating testing done in 1988. On April 21, 1988, Anastasio Cardinal Ballestrero of Turin supervised Italian micro-analyst Dr. Giovanni Riggi cutting a $\frac{1}{2}$ inch by 3 inch strip from the linen Shroud away from the central image or scorched areas, but from a corner site. The sample was then divided into three samples and given to the carbon dating laboratories at Zurich, Oxford, and the University of Arizona at Tucson, with each performing three radio carbon measurements.
>
> In October, the results were announced: the shroud was woven some time in between the years 1260 and 1390. [...] However, several scientists objected to the "infallible" pronouncements made by the laboratories.
>
> [now follows a list of possible pollution sources mentioned by Dr. Rosalie David of the Manchester Museum, and an equally futile

argument by Dr. Leoncio Garza-Valdes of the University of Texas, working with microbiologist Dr. Stephen Mattingly of the University of Texas Health Science Center at San Antonio]

[now follows the only possible physical mechanism, published in *Nature* in 1989 by Dr. Thomas J. Phillips of Harvard University High Energy Physics Laboratory: if the body had radiated neutrons during the act of resurrection, this would distort the measured carbon-dated age.]

In all, the preponderance of evidence appears to support the authenticity of the Shroud of Turin as the burial cloth of our Lord. The one "sticky" issue for most people which also blinds them to the rest of the evidence is the 1988 carbon dating evidence. While the Shroud is still not an article of faith, the Popes of our century, including his Holiness Pope John Paul II, see the Shroud as a relic that does aid our appreciation for what our Lord suffered for our salvation.

Dear reader, please bear my catholic straight comments to the above "catholic straight answers".

From back to front, the first comment relates to the last sentence. The Shroud's veracity as a proof of Christ's resurrection will *by definition* never be pronounced dogmatically, for the simple reason, that it concerns neither faith nor morality.

Second, all studies by well-intentioned catholic scientists looking for some kind of synthesis immediately end up in my trash bin. Why look for a synthesis with a lie? That is the stupidest one can possibly think of.[96]

The easiest way to explain the carbon dating results that Anastasio Cardinal Ballestrero thought that "supervising" the cutting process more or less ended his supervision duties. Well actually, my dear Anastasio, from that moment the supervision actually begins! *You should have made sure that every laboratory received 10 numbered but unknown samples.* What you allowed to happen, without heeding to STURP's multiple warnings, is that Michael Tite took full control. From that very moment, even the most illiterate Catholic would have known that everything was manipulated![97] Tite simply needed an uncertainty interval consistent with the 5730 years decay time of neutron decay, and consistent with the

---

96   Note that this remark does not apply to Thomas J. Phillips of Harvard University, as his work *assumes* Tite's conclusion to be wrong. I am only sorry for him taking seriously a hardly scientific result like Tite's.

97   As is common parlance among computer scientists: bull shit in, bull shit out.

arrival in 1307 of Jacques de Molay and his Lord-Relic in Paris. That is what Tite wanted, and that is what he got.

"Oh my dear, is your sample too old? Could you please wash it a bit more with product A to remove pollution?"

"Oh my dear, is your sample too young? Could you please wash it a bit more with product B to remove pollution?"

The reason Theism lost this battle against Deism is nothing else but episcopal stupidity.[98] That was already predicted by our Lord, so here you have a nice fulfillment of his prophecy, resulting in an overall 2-7 for deism versus theism.

---

98   How much more time should Christianity wait for an official report concerning the scientifically established veracity of the Holy Shroud? Nothing dogmatic, of course — just a lowest-level investigative report to world-wide Christianity on the scientifically closed topic of the Holy Shroud, eventually expanded with some theoretical babbling about the value of relics in general, as the motive of its publication. Oh yes, an explicit apology to STURP would not be superfluous, to say the least. John Paul the Great already told us about "self-purification of one's (historic) memory". Well, given that Anastasio Cardinal Ballestrero ruined the reputation of the Church with no reason, his actuation seems particularly fit in the list of errors committed by Catholics.

EPILOGUE
Match Point

Whatever funny dogmas were pronounced in the Catholic Church, they apparently did no harm to the investigative spirit of Catholic scientists. Still today, most ground-breaking solutions of unsolved problems are due to Catholic scientists. The Deists do not like that, however, and always tend to wipe out their names off science.

If they like it, let them do it. It does much more harm to the Deists themselves than to Catholicism as a whole. As I explained in this book the two lost points to Deism were due to the combination of Catholic ingenuousness and Deist fraudulence. Upon discarding these two false points to the real winner, the score ends at 0-9. Remember, this score regards the *nine most spectacular scientific feats* of the 20th century!

At this point I urge the reader to read the Wikipedia quote in the introduction again. Do you notice how vague that description is? I guess that, apart from some tiny points, even Catholicism fits under its definition!

The opposite does not hold, however. There is no way to encompass Deism as a branch of Catholicism. This is because of the Catholic dogmas. One such dogma concerns the existence of one God in three Persons.[99] These Persons have been revealed by the Christ as the Father, the Son (Himself), and the Holy Spirit.[100] Another such dogma is that the God is the Creator of Heaven and Earth. This single line, written down 2000 years ago, was enough to definitively prove the Catholic Church a fraud, *had Hoyle's Static Model reproduced the measured data.* However, Lemaître's model reproduced them time and again. Some ignorant fishermen of two millennia ago apparently saw the cosmological truth better than Einstein and Hoyle.

Yet another Catholic dogma states that God is infinitely superior to angels and humans, in all possible aspects. Had there not existed a Gödel-kind of

---

99   In philosophical terms, God refers to the one Essence
        common to the three Persons
100   God's Essence being of a strictly spiritual nature, neither
        "Father" nor "Son" have a sexual implication. God is sexless.
        This does not apply to the Second Person Incarnate, who was
        male, and had a natural mother. In Heaven, the Second
        Person will be sexless again, like all angels, and his Mother
        and us, too.

mathematical limit to mathematical human understanding, it would have proved the Catholic dogma of God's infinite superiority wrong. Had there not existed a Bell-kind of physical limit to physical human domination of nature, it would have proved the Catholic dogma of God's infinite superiority wrong twice. The same holds with respect to the creation of life, and of all living species. Evolutionists of the archaic school still believe everything is solved by the two buzzwords "variation" and "selection", but to date that is little more than a Buddhist mantra.

As long as nobody can explain the birth of the first cell, nobody is entitled to any declarations concerning the origin of mankind, which is a biological challenge possibly 1000 times harder to solve than that of the first self-replicating cell.

So let the evolutionists please go on with noisily preaching their ignorance of all matters biological. They merit a collective Darwin's award for loudly propagating scientific stupidities.

The only people scientifically more retrograde than evolutionists, are creationists, usually of protestant origin. How funny that both schools (evolutionism and creationism), so radically opposed to one another, are primarily inspired by their utter disdain of Catholicism! As far as the creationists are concerned, the main reasons for stepping out of the Catholic Church (an extremely inconsistent act) were: corruption of the Hierarchy, celibate, the Holy Eucharist, the Virgin Mother, Saints, dogma's, and some specific New-Testament quotes which were too overtly contradictory with their leaving the Church. Well, after more than two millennia of scientific investigation, none of these tenets (except corruption) have been proved contradictory. Meanwhile, they are presently busy digesting even bigger inconsistencies than their ancestors who left the Catholic Church.

www.ingramcontent.com/pod-product-compliance
Lightning Source LLC
Chambersburg PA
CBHW060322030426
42336CB00011B/1172